Madhur Jaffrey

Indian Cooking

BARRON'S

Madhur Jaffrey

Indian Cooking

BARRON'S

BBC

First edition for North America published in 2003
by Barron's Educational Series, Inc.

This edition first published in 2002.

© Madhur Jaffrey 2002
The moral right of the author has been asserted.

The recipes contained in this book first appeared in *Indian Cookery*, which was originally
published by BBC Books in 1982 and revised and updated in 1994 as *Madhur Jaffrey's
Illustrated Indian Cookery*.

Library of Congress Catalog Card No.: 2003102978

International Standard Book No.: 0-7641-5649-7

All inquiries should be addressed to:
Barron's Educational Series, Inc.
250 Wireless Boulevard
Hauppauge, New York 11788
http://www.barronseduc.com

Commissioning Editor: Nicky Copeland
Project Editor: Sarah Lavelle
Designer: Janet James
Art Director for jacket: Pene Parker
Production Controller: Christopher Tinker
New photography for this edition: Jean Cazals © Jean Cazals 2002
Home Economist: Marie Ange Lapierre
Stylist: Malika
Photography re-used from the 1994 edition: © James Murphy 1994;
Home Economist: Allyson Birch; Stylist: Jane McLish

The publishers would like to thank the following for supplying items used in the photographs:
Far Global Collection at Selfridges, Divertimenti, Verandah, Spice Islander, Southall Market,
Wigwam and Rupali.

Printed and bound in Singapore by Tien Wah Press
Jacket printed by Lawrence-Allen Ltd, Weston-super-Mare
Color separation by Kestrel Digital Colour, Chelmsford

9 8 7 6 5 4 3 2

contents

notes on the recipes

- Eggs are medium unless stated otherwise
- Wash all fresh produce before preparation
- Spoon measurements are level
- Conversions in the recipes are approximate and have been rounded up or down. Follow one set of measurements only; do not mix metric and imperial

LIQUID CONVERSIONS

1 tablespoon = 15 ml or 3 teaspoons

1 teaspoon = 5 ml

metric	imperial	US
10 ml	2 tsp	2 tsp
20 ml	1 tbsp	1½ tbsp
30 ml	1 fl oz	2 tbsp
60 ml	2 fl oz	¼ cup
125 ml	4 fl oz	½ cup
185 ml	6 fl oz	¾ cup
250 ml	8 fl oz	1 cup/½ pint
300 ml	10 fl oz/½ pint	1¼ cups
500 ml	16 fl oz	2 cups/1 pint
575 ml	20 fl oz/1 pint	2½ cups
1 litre	35 fl oz/1¾ pints	4½ cups

DRY/OTHER CONVERSIONS

As a general guide, regard 2 US teaspoons or tablespoons as 1 UK teaspoon or tablespoon.

1 dessertspoon is the equivalent of 2 teaspoons or half a tablespoon.

commodity	metric	imperial	cups
Butter/margarine	225 g	8 oz	1 cup
Breadcrumbs	90 g	3¼ oz	1 cup
Cheese (cheddar, parmesan, etc. grated)	50 g	2 oz	1 cup
Dried fruit (raisins, sultanas, etc.)	225 g	8 oz	1 cup
Flour (finely ground)	15 g	4 oz	1 cup
Coarse meals (semolina, oatmeal, etc.)	40 g	5 oz	1 cup
Nuts (almonds, hazelnuts, walnuts, etc.)	150 g	5½ oz	1 cup
Ground nuts	115 g	4 oz	1 cup
Rice (uncooked)	115 g	4 oz	1 cup
White sugar	225 g	8 oz	1 cup
Brown sugar	170 g	6 oz	1 cup
Confectioners' sugar	40 g	5 oz	1 cup
Molasses/syrup	350 g	12 oz	1 cup

preface

Nothing is more gratifying for any author than to have a book that has sold consistently well for over 20 years. Many young people come up to me today and say that they grew up on my food, cooked for them by their parents and that they are now cooking from my books for their children. It is enough to move me to tears.

When it was decided to do this latest "update" with fresh photographs, I found myself looking at my recipes again to see if they needed revising. They don't. They work just as well today as they did when I wrote them. What has changed is the world around us.

The day after I cooked Lemony Chicken with Fresh Coriander (page 95) on television in the 1980s, I was told that Manchester ran out of green coriander. This would not happen today. Even our supermarkets now are stocked with everything from fresh ginger and green chilies to okra. Basmati rice is sold universally, often in handy bags with zips, all cleaned and ready to go. Fully cooked *naans*, packaged to ensure freshness, can be had from neighborhood or specialty grocers to accompany a home-cooked Rogan Josh (page 70). Spice companies sell whole cumin and whole red chilies. This fills me with joy.

Even kitchen gadgets have moved along. It had been my dream to make a Japanese-style grater, perfect for ginger, universally available. It did not happen. Never mind. We now have the microplane grater. Fresh ginger moves on it like butter, providing a perfect "paste." You can even use it for large cloves of garlic. Garlic cloves have grown in size, haven't they? The little bits that are left can be collected and pushed through a garlic press. Cooking is becoming so much easier.

As the pace of life gets faster, many of us are turning, in our leisure hours, to ancient disciplines that help slow it down and give it perspective. Ayurveda is one of them. It tells us that simple kitchen acts like chopping, cutting, and grinding are graces that help calm the soul and bring it closer to its origins. Is that not what we are all searching for? Some think so.

When I first wrote *Indian Cookery*, Indian food was available mostly in second-rate restaurants at relatively cheap prices and considered the perfect accompaniment to mugs of beer or lager. While this is still true, two other things have happened. There is a better grade of restaurants, many serving regional foods, that have appeared, selling freshly cooked specialities. Also, there is a whole new generation of people cooking Indian food at home, from simple breakfast eggs to elaborate legs of lamb. They know better and are both knowledgeable and demanding. They may have gone to culinary schools. They may have traveled to India or have cook books to guide them. They are not easily fooled. They want authentic food. Good ingredients, properly cooked. This book is dedicated to them.

Madhur Jaffrey

introduction

I have always loved to eat well. My mother once informed me that my passion dates back to the hour of my birth when my grandmother wrote the sacred syllable "Om" ("I am") on my tongue with a finger dipped in fresh honey. I was apparently observed smacking my lips rather loudly.

Starting from that time, food – good food – just appeared miraculously from somewhere at the back of our house in Delhi. It would be preceded by the most tantalizing odors – steaming basmati rice, roasting cumin seeds, cinnamon sticks in hot oil – and the sounds of crockery and cutlery on the move. A bearer, turbaned, sashed, and barefoot, would announce the meal and soon we would all be sitting around the dinner table, a family of six, engrossed in eating monsoon mushrooms cooked with coriander and turmeric, *rahu* fish that my brothers had just caught in the Jamuna River, and cubes of lamb smothered in a yogurt sauce.

It was at this stage of innocence that I left India for London, to become a student at the Royal Academy of Dramatic Art. My "digs" were in Brent and consisted of a pleasant room and, through the kindness of my landlords, use of the kitchen.

"Use of the kitchen" was all very well, but exactly how was I going to use it? My visits to our kitchen in Delhi had been brief and intermittent. I could not cook. What was worse, I felt clumsy and ignorant.

An SOS to my mother brought in return a series of reassuring letters, all filled with recipes for my favorite foods. There they were, *Kheema matar* (Minced meat with peas), *Rogan josh* (Red lamb stew), *Phool gobi aur aloo ki bhaji* (Cauliflower with potatoes) …

Slowly, aided by the correspondence course with my encouraging mother, I did learn to cook, eventually getting cocky enough to invite large groups of friends over for meals of *Shahi korma* or *Shahjahani murghi* (Mughlai chicken with almonds and raisins). Once certain basic principles had been mastered, cooking Indian food had become perfectly accessible.

There is something so very satisfying about Indian cooking, more so when it is fresh and homemade. Perhaps it is that unique blending of herbs, spices, seasonings, as well as meat, pulses (see pages 162–175), vegetables, yogurt dishes, and relishes that my ancestors determined centuries ago would titillate our palates. At the same time it preserves our health and the proper chemical balance of our bodies. This combination of wholesome food and endless flavors and dishes makes Indian cooking one of the greatest in the world.

Indian food is far more varied than the menus of Indian restaurants suggest. One of my fondest memories of school in Delhi is of the lunches that we all brought from our homes, ensconced in

multitiered lunch boxes. My stainless steel lunch box used to dangle from my bicycle handlebar as I rode at great speed to school every morning, my ribboned pigtails fluttering behind me. The smells emanating from it sustained me as I dodged exhaust-spewing buses and, later, as I struggled with mind-numbing algebra. When the lunch bell finally set us free, my friends and I would assemble under a shady *neem* tree if it was summer or on a sunny verandah if it was winter. My mouth would begin to water even before we opened up our lunch boxes. It so happened that all my friends were of differing faiths and all came originally from different regions of the country. Even though we were all Indian, we had hardly any culinary traditions in common. Eating always filled us with a sense of adventure and discovery as we could not always anticipate what the others might bring.

My Punjabi friend was of the Sikh faith. She often brought large, round *parathas* made with wheat and *ghee* produced on her family farm. These were sometimes stuffed with tart pomegranate seeds and sometimes with cauliflower. We ate them with a sweet-and-sour, homemade turnip pickle.

Another friend was a Muslim from Uttar Pradesh, known to bring beef cooked with spinach, all deliciously flavored with chilies, cardamom, and cloves. Many of us were Hindus and not supposed to eat beef. So we just pretended not to know what it was. Our fingers would work busily around the tender meat that covered the bones and our cheeks would hollow as we sucked up the spicy marrow from the marrow bones. But we never asked what we were eating. The food was far too good for that. On the other hand, whenever my father went boar hunting and we cooked that meat at home, I never took it to school. I knew it would offend my Muslim friends.

Another member of our gang was a Jain from Gujerat. Jains are vegetarians, some of them so orthodox as to refrain from eating beets and tomatoes because their color reminds them of blood, and root vegetables because in pulling them out of the earth some innocent insect might have to lose its life. This friend occasionally brought the most delicious pancakes – *pooras* – made out of pulses.

One of us came from Kashmir, India's northernmost state. As she thrilled us with tales about tobogganing – the rest of us had never seen snow – she would unpack morel mushrooms from Kashmiri forests, cooked with tomatoes and peas and flavored with asafetida. This friend was a Hindu, of course. Only Kashmiri Hindus cook with asafetida. And they do not cook with garlic. Kashmiri Muslims cook with garlic and frown upon asafetida. I found all this much easier to follow than algebra.

We had a South Indian friend too, a Syrian Christian from Kerala. She often brought *idlis*, slightly sour, steamed rice cakes that we ate with *sambar*, a pulse, and fresh vegetable stew.

I, a Delhi Hindu, tried to dazzle my friends with quail and partridge that my father shot regularly and that our cook prepared with onions, ginger, cinnamon, black pepper, and yogurt.

India is such a large country – over a million square miles of changing topography, divided into thirty-one states and territories. Geography and local produce have played a great part in forming regional culinary traditions. Religious groups within each state have modified these regional cuisines even further to suit their own restrictions. History too, has had its influences. Goa, for example, on India's west coast, was ruled by the Portuguese for four centuries. Many of its people were converted to Catholicism, some by Saint Francis Xavier himself, and eventually developed an eating style that included platters of beef roulade – a stuffed roll of beef cooked in garlic-flavored olive oil – and a dessert of layered pancakes – *bibingka* – made with egg yolks, coconut milk, and raw Indian sugar. British colonialists left quite a few dishes in their wake too. There were those *cutlis* (cutlets) that our cook made. He, of course, marinated them in ginger and garlic first. Then, there was the strong influence of the Moguls. They had come to India via Persia in the sixteenth century and introduced the subcontinent to delicate *pullaos* and meats cooked with yogurt and fried onions.

If there is a common denominator in all Indian foods, it is, perhaps, the imaginative use of spices. Does this mean that Indian food is always spicy? Well, in a sense it does. It always uses spices, sometimes just one spice to cook a potato dish and sometimes up to fifteen spices to make an elaborate meat dish. But it is not always hot. The "heat" in Indian food comes from hot chilies. Chili peppers were introduced to Asia in the sixteenth century by the Portuguese who had discovered them in the New World. Our own pungent spices until that time were the more moderate mustard seeds and black peppercorns. Those of you who do not like hot food should just leave out all the chilies — red, green, or cayenne — in my recipes. Your food will still be authentically Indian, superb in flavor and not at all hot.

The spices and seasonings that we *do* like to use in our food include cumin, coriander, turmeric, black pepper, mustard seeds, fennel seeds, cinnamon, cardamom, and cloves. Sometimes we leave the spices whole and fry them, sometimes we roast the spices, and at other times we grind them and mix them with water or vinegar to make a paste. Each of these techniques draws out a completely different flavor from the same spice. This way we can give a great variety to, say, a vegetable like a potato, not only by methods such as boiling, baking, and roasting but by cooking it with whole cumin one time, a combination of ground cumin and roasted fennel seeds another time, and black pepper a third time. The permutations become endless as does the possibility of variety in tastes.

Does this mean that you cannot cook Indian food without having a whole lot of spices? I suggest that you start off by buying the specific spices you need to cook a selected dish and then slowly increase your spice "wardrobe." It is a bit like being a painter, I suppose. If you have a palette glowing with magenta and cobalt blue and sap green and vermilion, it will give you the confidence — and the choice — to do anything you want. You could use one color, if you desired, or ten. It is the same with spices. It is nice to know that they are there. Whole spices last a long time. This way, you can cook eggplant with fennel seeds one day and green beans with cumin seeds the next day, if that is what you want.

Once you have mastered the use of Indian spices, you will find yourself not only cooking Indian meals but also inventing dishes with an Indian flavor and using Indian spices in unexpected ways. A French chef who once observed me cooking, now regularly uses ground roasted cumin seeds in his cream of tomato soup. I myself have created an Indian-style dish of pork chipolatas for this book to start you off in this pleasant direction. So don't be afraid to experiment — and have fun!

spices, seasonings, and flavorings

Many of the spices used in Indian foods can be found in supermarkets. These include cumin, coriander, turmeric, cloves, cinnamon, cardamom, nutmeg, black pepper, bay leaves, ginger, paprika, and cayenne pepper. Others have to be sought out from delicatessens and Greek, Indian, or Pakistani grocers. Such grocers can be found in all major cities and in many small towns as well. It is also possible to order spices by mail and on the Internet.

Ideally speaking, it is best to buy all dry spices in their whole form. They will stay fresh for long periods if stored in cool, dry, dark places in tightly covered jars. This way you can grind the spices as you need them. I use an electric coffee grinder for this purpose, although a pestle and mortar would do. The more freshly ground the spices, the better their flavor. If you can only buy ground spices, buy small quantities and store them, too, in cool, dry, dark places in tightly covered jars.

When transferring spices from plastic bags to jars, be sure to label them. When buying spices from ethnic grocers, make sure that they are labeled. Many of my cooking students have come to me with unlabeled jars and asked, "What do I have here?" Even I, who have been cooking now for more than thirty years, cannot tell the difference between ground cumin and ground coriander without tasting or smelling them first.

Here is a list of the spices, seasonings, and flavorings used in this book.

AMCHOOR Green Mango Powder

Unripe, sour, green mangoes are sliced and dried in the sun. Indian grocers sell both the dried slices and ground *amchoor*. Only the ground version is called for in this book. *Amchoor* is one of the many souring agents used in Indian cuisine. The powder can get lumpy so crush it well between your fingers before sprinkling it over foods.

ASAFETIDA Heeng

The Indian source for this smelly resin has traditionally been Afghanistan and western Kashmir. In its lump form, asafetida looks rather like the brown rosin my husband uses on the bow of his violin. Its smell is another matter. James Beard, America's foremost food writer, once compared the smell to that of fresh truffles. This seasoning is a digestive and is used in very small quantities. (It can even cure horses of indigestion!) A pinch of it is thrown into very hot oil and allowed to fry for a second before other foods are added. As asafetida is not widely available in supermarkets, I have made its use optional in most of my recipes. If you wish to purchase it, I suggest that you buy the smallest box available of *ground* asafetida. Make sure that the cover sits tightly on the box when you store it.

Clockwise from top left: Ground cardamom seed, cardamom pods, and whole cardamom seed

CARDAMOM, PODS, AND SEEDS Elaichi

Cardamom pods are whitish or green and have parchment-like skins and lots of round, black, highly aromatic seeds inside. The whitish pods are more readily available in supermarkets. They have been bleached and have less flavor and aroma than the unbleached green ones. For my recipes, use whichever pods you can find easily, although the green ones are better.

Many of my recipes call for whole pods. They are used as a flavoring in both savory and sweet dishes. When used whole, cardamom pods are not meant to be eaten. We leave them on the side of the plate, along with any bones. When a recipe calls for cardamom *seeds*, you can either take the seeds out of the pods (a somewhat tedious task, best done while watching television) or else you can buy the seeds from the few Indian and Pakistani grocers who sell them. If my recipe calls for a small amount of *ground* cardamom seeds, pulverize them in a mortar.

CAYENNE PEPPER Pisi hui lal mirch

Made from dried red chilies, this is called red chili powder by Indian and Pakistani grocers. Most of my recipes have a flexible amount of cayenne pepper in them. It is hard to know how hot people like their food. Use the smaller amount if you want your food just mildly hot and the larger amount if you want it hotter.

CHILIES, FRESH, HOT, GREEN Hari mirch

These fresh chilies, 5–10 cm (2–4 inches) long, green outside, and filled with flat round, white seeds, are rich in vitamins A and C. They give Indian foods a very special flavor.

Green chilies should be stored unwashed and wrapped in newspaper, in a plastic container in the refrigerator. Any chilies that go bad should be thrown away as they affect the whole batch.

Note: Be careful when handling cut green chilies. Refrain from touching your eyes or your mouth; wash your hands as soon as possible, otherwise you will "burn" your skin with the irritant the chilies contain. If you want the green chili flavor without most of the heat, remove the white seeds.

Above:
Cayenne pepper

CHILIES, DRIED, HOT, RED Sabut lal mirch

These chilies, about 4–5 cm (1½ –2 inches) long and 7 mm–1 cm (⅓ –½ inches) wide, are often thrown into hot oil for a few seconds until they puff up and their skin darkens. This fried skin adds its own very special flavor to a host of meats, vegetables, and pulses. Handle these chilies carefully, making sure that you wash your hands well before you touch your face. If you want the flavor of the chilies without their heat, make a small opening in them and then shake out and discard their seeds.

CINNAMON Dar cheeni

We often use cinnamon sticks whole in meat and rice dishes. They are used just for their flavor and aroma and are not meant to be eaten.

CLOVES, WHOLE Long

We often use whole cloves in our meat and rice dishes for their flavor and aroma. They are not meant to be eaten. (It must be added that we do suck on cloves as a mouth freshener.)

COCONUT, FRESH GRATED Nariyal

When buying coconuts, make sure that they are crack-free and have no mold on them. Shake them to make sure that they are heavy with liquid. Now hold a coconut in one hand over a sink and hit it around the center with the claw end of a hammer or with the blunt side of a heavy cleaver. The coconut should crack and break into two halves. (You could, if you like, collect the liquid in a cup. It is not used in cooking, but you may drink it. I do. I consider it my reward for breaking open the coconut in the first place.) Taste a piece of the coconut to make sure it is sweet and not rancid. Peel off the coconut flesh from the hard shell with a knife. If it proves to be too obstinate and you have a gas stove, it helps to put the coconut halves, cut side up, directly over a low flame, turning them around now and then so they char slightly. The woody shell contracts and releases the kernel.

Now peel off the brown coconut skin with a potato peeler and break the flesh into 2.5 cm- (1 inch-) pieces (larger ones if you are grating manually). Wash off these coconut pieces and either grate them finely on a hand grater or else put them in an electric blender or food processor. Do not worry about turning them into pulp in these electric machines. What you will end up with will be very finely "grated" coconut, perfect for all the Indian dishes that require it. Grated coconut freezes beautifully and defrosts fast. I always grate large quantities whenever I have the time and store it in the freezer for future use.

COCONUT MILK

Coconut milk is made by grating coconut, mixing it with water and then squeezing out the juice. Since coconuts in the West vary so much in their freshness, I find it much easier to use a good brand of canned coconut milk. I like Chaokoh, which is a Thai brand. The cream in coconut milk rises to the top of the can so follow the recipe directions regarding stirring or not stirring its contents.

CORIANDER, FRESH GREEN OR CILANTRO Hara dhaniya or kothmir

This is one of India's favorite herbs and is used, just as parsley might be, both as a garnish and for its flavor. This pretty green plant grows about 15–20 cm (6–8 inches) in height. Just the top, leafy section is used, though the stems are sometimes thrown into pulse dishes for their aroma.

To store fresh green coriander, put it in its unwashed state, roots and all, into a container filled with water, almost as if you were putting flowers in a vase. The leafy section of the plant should not be in water. Put a plastic bag over the coriander and container and refrigerate. The fresh coriander should last for weeks. Every other day, pick off and discard yellowing leaves. Parsley can be used as a substitute.

CORIANDER SEEDS, WHOLE AND GROUND Dhania, sabut, and pisa

These are the round, beige seeds of the coriander plant. They are used a lot in Indian cooking, generally in their ground form. You may buy them already ground, or you could buy the whole seeds and grind them yourself in small quantities in an electric coffee grinder. I like to put my home-ground coriander seeds through a strainer though this is not essential.

Ground coriander seeds, if stored for several months, begin to taste a little like sawdust. It is best to discard them at this stage and start off with a fresh batch.

Right:
Coriander seeds (top)
and cloves (bottom)

Clockwise from top:
Fennel seeds,
cumin seeds,
fenugreek seeds
(right), and mustard
seeds (left)

CUMIN SEEDS, WHOLE AND GROUND Zeera, sabut and pisa

These carawaylike seeds are used very frequently in Indian food, both in their whole and ground forms. Whole seeds keep their flavor much longer than ground ones and may be ground very easily in an electric coffee grinder.

ROASTED CUMIN SEEDS: Put 4–5 tablespoons of whole cumin seeds into a small, heavy frying pan (cast-iron frying-pans are best for this) and place the pan over medium heat. No fat is necessary. Stir the seeds and keep roasting them until they turn a few shades darker. Soon you will be able to recognize the wonderful "roasted" aroma that these seeds emit when they are ready. Store in an airtight container.

GROUND, ROASTED CUMIN SEEDS: Empty the roasted seeds into an electric coffee grinder or other spice grinder and grind them finely. You could also use a pestle and mortar for this or else put the seeds between two sheets of brown paper and crush them with a rolling pin. Store ground, roasted cumin seeds in a tightly covered jar.

CUMIN SEEDS, BLACK Shah zeera or kala zeera

These fine seeds are darker and more expensive than regular cumin seeds. They look like caraway seeds but have a gentle flavor. Buy them whole. If you cannot find them, use regular cumin seeds as a substitute.

FENNEL SEEDS Sonf

These seeds taste and look like anise seeds only they are larger, plumper, and milder. They give meat and vegetables a delicious, liquoricelike flavor. Indians often serve roasted fennel seeds at the end of a meal as a digestive and mouth freshener.

FENUGREEK SEEDS Methi

These yellow, square seeds are used sparingly as they have a strong, earthy odor. They are used in pickling, curry powders, and vegetarian dishes.

GARAM MASALA

This is an aromatic mixture that generally incorporates spices that are supposed to heat the body (the words mean "hot spices") such as large black cardamoms, cinnamon, black cumin (also called *shah zeera* or royal cumin), cloves, black peppercorns, and nutmeg. The mixture is used sparingly and is generally put into foods toward the end of their cooking period. It is also used as a garnish — a final aromatic flavoring sprinkled over cooked meats, vegetables, and pulses.

Garam masala is not a standardized spice mixture. Apart from the fact that there are many regional variations, I am sure that every north Indian and Pakistani home has its own family recipe. The recipe here happens to be one of my favorites. I have substituted seeds from the green cardamom pods for the more traditional black ones as I find their taste to be far more delicate.

Indian and Pakistani grocers and most supermarkets do sell a ready-made *garam masala* that you may certainly resort to in emergencies. However, you will find it quite pallid, as cheaper spices such as cumin and coriander are often substituted for the more expensive cardamom and cloves.

It is best to grind *garam masala* in small quantities so that it stays fresh. My recipe makes about 3 tablespoons.

1 tablespoon cardamom seeds

5 cm (2 inch)-cinnamon stick

1 teaspoon black cumin seeds (use regular cumin seeds as a substitute)

1 teaspoon cloves

1 teaspoon black peppercorns

¼ average-sized nutmeg

Place all the ingredients in a clean, electric coffee grinder (or any other spice grinder). Turn the machine on for 30–40 seconds or until the spices are finely ground. Store in a small jar with a tight-fitting cover.

Remember to keep it away from heat and sunlight.

Right:
Fresh ginger

GINGER, DRIED GROUND Sonth

This is ginger that is dried and powdered, the same you might use to make gingerbread.

GINGER, FRESH Adrak

This light brown, knobbly "root" is not a root at all but a rhizome with a refreshing, pungent flavor. Its potatolike skin needs to be peeled away before it can be chopped, sliced, grated, or made into a paste. To grate ginger into a pulp, use a microplane grater or the finest part of a plain hand grater. To grind ginger into a paste, chop it coarsely first and then throw it into the container of a food processor or blender. Add just enough water to make as smooth a paste as possible.

When buying ginger, look for pieces that are not too wrinkled but have a taut skin. If you use ginger infrequently, "store" ginger by planting it in a somewhat dry, sandy soil. Water it infrequently. Your ginger will not only survive, but will also sprout fresh knobs. Whenever you need some, dig it up, break off a knob, and then plant the rest again. If you use ginger frequently, store it in a cool, airy basket, along with your onions, potatoes, and garlic.

KALONJI Nigella

This spice is a small, black, teardrop-shaped onion seed with an appealing earthy aroma. It is used for cooking vegetable and fish dishes in Bengal. The rest of the country uses it for pickling. Some north Indian breads such as *naans* have these seeds sprinkled on them before they are baked. *Kalonji* is sold in Indian and Pakistani stores.

KEWDA ESSENCE

This flowery essence comes from a variety of the screw-pine plant. In Muslim Indian cooking it is used in banquet-style dishes of rice and meat and in desserts. It may even be sprinkled on breads though this is usually done not with the concentrated essence but with the lighter *kewda* water that is sold in larger bottles. *Kewda* is also available as a syrup that is mixed with ice and water to make a summer drink.

MUSTARD OIL Sarson ka tel

This yellow oil made from mustard seeds is quite pungent when raw and amazingly sweet when heated to a slight haze. It is used in Bengal and Kashmir for cooking vegetables and fish. It is the favorite oil throughout India for pickling. It is available at Indian and Pakistani grocers. If you cannot find it, groundnut oil may be substituted.

MUSTARD SEEDS, WHOLE BLACK Sarson

Once you start using these seeds, you will not want to stop. They are round, tiny, and not really black but a dark reddish brown color. When scattered into hot oil they turn deliciously nutty. If you want to know what they taste like alone, make the Gujerati Carrot Salad on page 217. They are the main seasoning in that dish. Mustard seeds are now widely available.

NUTMEG Jaiphal

Buy whole nutmegs. If a recipe calls for a third of a nutmeg, just hit a nutmeg lightly with a hammer. It is very soft and breaks quite easily.

POPPY SEEDS, WHITE Khaskhas

Poppy seeds can be blue or white. India just happens to grow the white ones. These very tiny seeds are usually roasted first and then ground to make a nutty paste that is excellent in meat sauces. It thickens the sauces and provides a deeper flavor at the same time. When used in kebabs and meatballs it adds a touch of firmness just as breadcrumbs might.

SAFFRON Zaafraan or kesar

Saffron threads are the stigma of special crocuses that, in India, grow in the northern state of Kashmir. Saffron is expensive. It is used in festive dishes both for its saffron color and its aroma. Yellow food coloring, or a small pinch of turmeric, may be substituted for the real thing even though purists would disapprove.

To get the most color and flavor out of saffron, Indians often roast the threads lightly in a heavy cast-iron frying pan and then crumble them into a small amount of hot milk. This milk is then poured into rice and meat dishes as well as desserts.

Saffron is sold in some supermarkets, all fine delicatessens, and most Indian and Pakistani grocers. Powdered saffron is also available in selected shops.

SALT

Amounts of salt given in recipes can be adjusted to suit individual tastes.

SESAME SEEDS Til

I use the beige, unhulled seeds that are sold in all health food stores and at all oriental grocers. They have a wonderful, nutty flavor, especially after they have been roasted.

TURMERIC Haldi

This is the spice that makes many Indian foods yellow. Apart from its mild, earthy flavor, it is used mainly because it is a digestive and an antiseptic. Fresh turmeric looks like the baby sister of fresh ginger. They are both rhizomes. Buy the ground kind. Use it carefully as it can stain.

VARAK

This airy, real-silver tissue is used for garnishing sweets as well as festive meat and rice dishes. It is sold only at some Indian and Pakistani grocers. Each silver tissue is packed between sheets of paper. Remove the top sheet carefully. Then pick up the next sheet with the *varak* on it and overturn it gently on the food you wish to garnish. Try not to let the *varak* disintegrate. It is edible. Store it in a tightly closed tin as it can tarnish.

VEGETABLE OIL

Most of my recipes call, rather generally, for vegetable oil. You could use what is labeled as vegetable oil in the supermarkets or you could use groundnut oil, corn oil, sunflower oil, or simple olive oil. All would be quite suitable.

YELLOW AND RED FOOD COLORINGS

These are used on some Indian foods – for instance these give *tandoori* food its distinctive coloring. They are vegetable colorings and have no taste. However, one word of warning: a few people (and that includes me!) are allergic to the tartrazine contained in these colorings.

Opposite: Turmeric

equipment

If you are going to cook authentic Indian food, do you need any special kitchen equipment? For those of you who already have well-equipped kitchens, the answer is probably "no." Good knives, sturdy pots with a good distribution of heat, rolling pins, graters, bowls, slotted spoons, pestle and mortar, frying pans — I am sure you have these already. There are, however, a few items that make the cooking of Indian food simpler.

AN ELECTRIC FOOD PROCESSOR OR BLENDER Every Indian home has a grinding stone. This consists of a large, flat stone that just sits and a smaller stone that is moved manually on top of it and does the grinding. These stones are exceedingly heavy. It is just as well that they are no longer essential. Their place, in modern kitchens, can be taken by food processors and blenders. Onions, garlic, and ginger, formerly ground on grinding stones, can now be made into a paste in electrically powered machines.

If you do not have a food processor or blender, then there are ways around it. Garlic, for example, can be mashed in a mortar or put through a garlic press. Ginger can be grated on the finest part of the grater. Onions can just be chopped very finely. Sometimes my recipe suggests putting water into the food processor while making the paste. If you have crushed the garlic and grated the ginger by hand, just put them into a bowl and add the amount of water in the recipe.

If you decide to go out and buy a blender, make sure that its blades sit close to the bottom, otherwise it will not pulverize small quantities adequately.

MICROPLANE GRATER This is the best gadget I have found for grating fresh, peeled ginger to a pulp.

AN ELECTRIC COFFEE GRINDER Food processors and blenders cannot do all the work of an Indian grinding stone. Dry spices, for example, cannot be ground in them properly. For this, only a coffee grinder will do. A coffee grinder grinds spices in seconds and can then be wiped clean. If you do not have one, you will have to crush your spices in small quantities with a pestle and mortar.

TONGS My favorite tongs are intended for barbecues but I use them for turning chicken pieces, picking up meat pieces when they are browning, and even for tossing a salad.

A LARGE NONSTICK FRYING PAN WITH A COVER Nonstick pans really take the worry out of cooking many foods. Browning meats do not stick to the bottom, nor do sauces with ginger or almonds. As metal spoons ruin the finish of nonstick utensils, it is best to have a set of plastic or wooden ones.

SMALL AND LARGE CAST-IRON FRYING PANS I keep a 13 cm (5 inch)-cast-iron frying pan for roasting spices – it can heat without oil or water in it – and for doing *baghaar*, frying small amounts of spices in oil. A larger cast-iron pan is excellent for making Indian breads such as *parathas* and *chapatis*. In India, these breads are cooked on a *tava*, a round, concave cast-iron plate. A large cast-iron frying pan makes the best substitute.

KARHAI This is very similar to a Chinese wok. If you took a large, hollow ball and cut it in half, that would be about the shape of a *karhai*. I am not suggesting that you go out and buy a *karhai*. I just wish to point out that for deep-frying it is perhaps the most economical utensil, as it allows you to use a relatively small quantity of oil while giving you enough depth in the center of the utensil to submerge foods. A deep frying pan can be substituted for a *karhai*.

ELECTRIC RICE COOKERS If you frequently cook large quantities of rice, an electric rice cooker can be a useful piece of equipment. The cooker has a large covered pan that sits on top of an electric element. When the water has been absorbed by the rice the cooker switches itself off, and will then keep the rice warm for several hours. The preparation of the rice and the amount of water you use are identical to the conventional methods of cooking rice.

techniques

Indian food is unique in its imaginative use of spices, seasonings, and flavorings. Many of our cooking techniques are really ways of getting these same spices, seasonings, and flavorings to yield as great a variety of tastes and textures as possible. Spices and herbs do not have single, limited tastes. Depending upon how they are used – whole, ground, roasted, fried – they can be coaxed into producing a much larger spectrum than you might first imagine. Herein lies the genius of Indian cooking.

It amuses me to find that many of the techniques used in nouvelle cuisine have been used in India for centuries. We are told that sauces can be made much lighter if they are thickened with ingredients other than flour. Flour is almost never used as a thickener for Indian sauces. Instead, we have used, very cleverly, I might add, ingredients such as onions, garlic, ginger, yogurt, and tomatoes.

I think it might be useful, before you actually start cooking a recipe from this book, to measure and prepare all the ingredients you need for the recipe and have them ready near the stove. Once you are experienced, this will not matter as much. But for those of you who are new to Indian cooking, it will help if you make all your pastes and do all your chopping and measuring before you start. The reason for this is that many Indian dishes require you to cook in one, flowing sweep. Ingredient follows ingredient, often swiftly. Frequently there is no time to stop and hunt for a spice that is hidden in the back of a cupboard. Something on the stove might burn if you do. So organize yourself and read the recipe carefully. If many of the ingredients go into the pan at the same time, you can measure them out and keep them in the same bowl or plate.

Here are some of the more commonly used techniques.

CLARIFYING BUTTER Ghee: Not all Indian food is cooked in *ghee*, as some people imagine. Many of our foods are *meant* to be cooked in vegetable oil. But *ghee* does have a rich, nutty taste and a spoonful of it is frequently put on top of cooked pulses to enrich them and give them a silky smoothness. I must add here that there are certain families in India (not ours) who have always cooked in *ghee*. There used to be a certain amount of status attached to being able to say, "We use nothing but pure *ghee*." But today, even these families are coming around to using unsaturated fats.

I feel that cooking in *ghee* is a bit like cooking in butter. It is fine to do it some of the time for certain selected dishes. Some of my recipes do call for *ghee*. I suggest you buy it, ready-made, from Asian grocers. However, if you wish to make it yourself, melt 450 g (1 lb) unsalted butter in a small, heavy pot over low heat. Then let it simmer very gently for 10–30 minutes. The length of the time will depend upon the amount of water in the butter. As soon as the white, milky residue turns to golden particles (you have to keep watching), strain the *ghee* through several layers of cheesecloth or a large handkerchief. Cool and then pour into a clean jar. Cover. Properly made *ghee* does not need refrigeration.

DROPPING SPICES INTO HOT OIL Baghaar: I do not know of this technique being used anywhere else in the world. Oil (or *ghee*) is heated until it is extremely hot, but not burning. Then spices, generally whole ones, or else chopped-up garlic and ginger, are added to the oil. The seasonings immediately begin to swell, brown, pop, or otherwise change character. This seasoned oil, together with all the spices in it, is then poured over cooked foods such as pulses and vegetables or else uncooked foods are added to it and are then sautéed or simmered. The seasonings that are most commonly used for *baghaar* include cumin seeds, black mustard seeds, fennel seeds, dried red chilies, cloves, cinnamon sticks, cardamom pods, bay leaves, and black peppercorns as well as chopped-up garlic and ginger. Hot oil transforms them all and gives them a new, more concentrated character. When the whole spices used are large, such as bay leaves, cinnamon sticks, or even cloves and peppercorns, they are not meant to be eaten but are left to one side of the plate.

**Above:
Spices dropped
into hot oil**

GRINDING SPICES Many recipes call for ground spices. In India, we generally buy our spices whole and then grind them ourselves as and when we need them. They have much more flavor this way. You probably already know the difference between freshly ground black pepper and ground pepper that has been sitting around for a month. The same applies to all spices. In India, the grinding of spices is generally done on heavy grinding stones. We, in our modern kitchens, can get the same results without the labor by using an electric coffee grinder. It is best to grind limited quantities so that the spices do not lose their flavor. If you wipe the grinder carefully after use there will be no aftertaste of spices to flavor your coffee beans.

Buying ground spices is perfectly all right as long as you know that they will be less potent as time goes on. Before buying your spices, consult the preceding chapter to see which spices you must buy whole and which you may buy ground.

ROASTING SPICES This brings out yet another flavor from the spices. In my home, for example, we always make yogurt relishes with cumin that has been roasted first and then ground. Nothing else will do. Ordinary ground cumin has a different flavor, quite unsuitable for putting into foods that are not going to be cooked. This roasting is best done in a heavy, cast-iron frying pan since the pan can be heated without putting oil or water into it first. Whole spices are put into the pan. The pan is then shaken around until the spices turn a shade or two darker and emit their new "roasted" aroma. You will begin to recognize it after you have done it a few times.

MAKING THICK SAUCES Many of our meat, poultry, and fish dishes have thick, dark sauces. My mother always said that the mark of a good chef was his or her sauce, which depended not only on a correct balance of all the ingredients, but also on the correct frying (*bhuno*-ing) of these ingredients.

As I stated earlier, there is no flour in these sauces. The "body" comes, very often, from onions, garlic, and ginger. The rich brown color comes from frying all these ingredients properly. Very often, we make a paste of one or more of these ingredients first. In India, this is done on a grinding stone but in Western kitchens it can be done easily in food processors and blenders, sometimes with the aid of a little water.

Once the paste has been made, it needs to be browned or the sauce will not have the correct flavor and color. This is best done in a heavy pot or pan, preferably nonstick, in a *generous* amount of oil. Remember that extra oil can always be spooned off the top once the dish has been cooked.

BROWNING SLICED OR CHOPPED ONIONS AND GARLIC Sometimes a recipe requires that you brown thinly sliced or chopped onions. I have noticed that many of the students in my cooking classes stop halfway and when I point out to them that the onions are not quite done, they say, "Oh, but if we cook them more, they will burn." They will not, not if you watch. Start the frying on medium-high heat and turn the heat down somewhat as the onions lose their water and begin to turn brown. They do need to be a rich reddish brown color or your sauce — if that is what they are intended for — will be pale and weak.

The same goes for garlic. There is a common misconception that if garlic is allowed to pick up any color at all, it will turn bitter. Actually, garlic tastes quite superb if it is chopped and allowed to fry in oil until it turns a medium-brown color. I often cook zucchini this way — in oil that has been flavored with browned garlic. Spinach and cauliflower taste good this way too. In India, we say that such dishes are cooked with a garlic *baghaar*. A garlic *baghaar* can, of course, just be the first step in a recipe. More spices would be added later.

ADDING YOGURT TO SAUCES Yogurt adds a creamy texture and a delicate tartness to many of our sauces. But yogurt curdles when it is heated. So when we add it to our browning sauces, we add just 1 tablespoon at a time. After a tablespoon of yogurt has been put in, it is stirred and fried until it is absorbed and "accepted" by the sauce. Then the next tablespoon is added.

PEELING AND CHOPPING TOMATOES Many of my recipes call for peeled and chopped tomatoes. To peel them, bring a pan of water to a rolling boil. Drop in the tomatoes for 15 seconds. Drain, rinse under cold water, and peel. Now chop the tomatoes, making sure that you save all the juice that comes out of them. In India, we very rarely seed tomatoes. Many people do not even bother to peel them though I do feel that this improves the texture of a sauce.

REDUCING SAUCES Sometimes meat is allowed to cook in a fairly thin, brothy sauce. Then the lid of the pan is removed and the sauce reduced over fairly high heat until it is thick and clings to the meat. The meat has to be stirred frequently at this stage, so that it does not catch and burn.

COOKING CHICKEN WITHOUT ITS SKIN In India, we almost always remove the skin of the chicken before we cook it. The flavor of the spices penetrates the chicken much better this way and the entire dish is less fatty. It is very easy to remove the skin. Just hold it with a paper towel so that it does not slip, and pull!

MARINATING We often cut deep slashes in large pieces of meat and leave them overnight in a marinade of yogurt and seasonings. The yogurt tenderizes the meat while the slashes allow the flavor to penetrate deep inside the meat. After this, the meat can be grilled or baked faster than usual.

BROWNING MEATS In India, we generally do not brown cubes of meat by themselves but brown them with the sauce instead. However, in the West many meats release far too much water as they cook – Indian meats tend to be very fresh and have far less water in them. So to avoid this problem I brown my meat a few pieces at a time in hot oil and set them aside. Once I have made the sauce, I add the browned meat cubes (and all the good juices that come out of them) and let them cook.

These are just a few of the techniques that we use in Indian cookery. Others, that have to do with cooking rice or pulses, are dealt with in the relevant chapters.

Above:
Marinating chicken

menus
AND HOW TO EAT INDIAN FOOD

What do you eat with what? I have suggested accompaniments for the recipes in this book. You do not have to follow my suggestions. After all, the fun of eating is to follow your own palate and put together dishes that are convenient and exciting for you.

Generally speaking, an Indian meal consists of a meat dish, a vegetable dish, bread and/or rice, a pulse dish, a yogurt relish (or plain yogurt), and a fresh chutney or small, relishlike salad. Pickles and preserved chutneys may be added if you have them. Fruit rather than desserts is served at the end of a meal, although on festive occasions sweets would not be at all amiss. Sometimes, when the meat dish is particularly elegant and rich, we eliminate the pulse and serve an equally elegant *pullao* rice. Vegetarians — of whom there are millions in India — increase the number of vegetable and pulse dishes and always serve yogurt in some form.

Within this general framework, we try to see that the dishes we serve vary in color, texture, and flavor. If the meat, for example, has a lot of sauce, then we often serve a "dry," unsauced vegetable with it. If the vegetable we are serving is very soft — such as spinach — we make sure that there is a crunchy relish on the table.

Most Indians like to eat with their hands. The more Westernized ones may use knives and forks or spoons and forks, or just forks, but they too succumb every now and then to the pleasure of eating with their fingers.

It is only the right hand that is used for eating, the left being considered "unclean." With it, we break pieces of bread and then use the pieces to scoop up some meat or vegetable. With it, we also form neat

morsels out of rice and other accompanying dishes and then transport them to our mouths. In the northern states such as Uttar Pradesh, this is done very delicately with just the tips of the fingers. In the south, almost the entire hand may be used. Needless to say, hands must be washed before and after eating. Even the humblest of roadside stalls catering to simple villagers and truck drivers would not consider offering food before offering a *lota* (water vessel) of water for washing first.

When we serve ourselves, we put most foods beside each other on our plates. Only very wet, flowing dishes are sometimes ladled on top of the rice but not on top of *all* the rice. Some of the rice is left plain to enable us to eat it with other dishes. Very wet dishes that are meant to be eaten with bread are served in small, individual bowls.

This is all very well if you are cooking a whole Indian meal. If you feel like making such a meal, then by all means, do it. On the other hand, there is no reason why you cannot serve an Indian vegetable with your roast lamb or eat an Indian meat (such as Chicken in a Butter Sauce, page 92) with French bread and a salad. If you are on a diet, you could make yourself a Yogurt with Cucumber and Mint (page 210) for lunch and follow it with a crunchy apple. I have even served a roast leg of lamb with Black-eyed Beans with Mushrooms (page 174), Simple Buttery Rice with Onion (page 194), and a green salad. It is an easy meal to put together *and* it is good.

suggested menus

Here are some suggestions for a variety of delicious meals for everyday eating or entertaining.

Serves 6

Mughlai Lamb with Turnips, *Shabdeg* (page 75)

Mushroom Pullao, *Khumbi pullao* (page 199)

Spicy Green Beans, *Masaledar sem* (page 132)

Yogurt with Cucumber and Mint, *Kheere ka raita* (page 210)

Serves 4

Shrimp in a Dark Sauce, *Rasedar jhinga* (page 119)

Plain Basmati Rice, *Basmati chaaval* (page 193)

Cauliflower with Potatoes, *Phool gobi aur aloo ki bhaji* (page 144)

Tomato, Onion, and Cilantro Relish, *Cachumber* (page 215)

Serves 6

Black-eyed Beans with Mushrooms, *Lobhia aur khumbi* (page 174)

Cauliflower with Onion and Tomato, *Phool gobi ki bhaji* (page 142)

Layered Bread, *Paratha* (page 179)

Gujerati Carrot Salad, *Gajar ka salad* (page 217)

Serves 4–6

Beef Baked with Yogurt and Black Pepper, *Dum gosht* (page 69)

Eggplant Cooked in the Pickling Style, *Baigan achari* (page 136)

Rice and Peas, *Tahiri* (page 196)

Tomato, Onion, and Cilantro Relish, *Cachumber* (page 215)

Serves 4

Cod Steaks in a Spicy Tomato Sauce, *Timatar wali macchi* (page 122)

South Indian-style Light, Fluffy Rice, *Dakshini chaaval* (page 193)

Spicy Cucumber Wedges, *Kheere ke tukray* (page 218)

Serves 6

Shahjahani Leg of Lamb, *Shahjahani raan* (page 78)

Aromatic Yellow Rice, *Peelay chaaval* (page 200)

Green Beans with Ginger and Cilantro, *Hare masale ki sem* (page 133)

Drunken Orange Slices, *Sharabi narangi* (page 225)

Serves 6

Turkey Kebabs, *Turkey ke kabab* (page 104)

Potatoes with Black Pepper, *Bengali aloo* (page 153)

Cabbage with Peas, *Bund gobi aur matar* (page 140)

Naan (page 184) or store-bought pita bread

Serves 4

Chicken with Roasted Coriander in a Coconut Curry Sauce, *Dakshini murgh* (page 102)

Fried Eggplant Slices, *Tala hua baigan* (page 134)

Spiced Basmati Rice, *Masaledar basmati* (page 194)

Semolina Halva, *Sooji ka halva* (page 226)

Serves 6

Mughlai Chicken with Almonds and Raisins, *Shahjahani murghi* (page 96)

Plain Basmati Rice, *Basmati chaaval* (page 193)

Moong Dal and Red Lentils with Browned Onions, *Mili moong aur masoor dal* (page 170)

"Dry" Okra, *Sookhi bhindi* (page 152)

Serves 4

Salmon Steamed with Crushed Mustard Seeds and Tomato, *Salmon bhapey* (page 124)

Simple Buttery Rice with Onion, *Pyaz wali basmati chaaval* (page 194)

Whole Green Lentils with Spinach and Ginger (page 168)

Mixed Vegetables in a Mustard and Cumin Sauce, *Shorvedar subzi* (page 158)

Indians love to munch. Whether they are on buses or trains, in cinemas or in parks, they can be spotted opening up newspaper cones, unwrapping dish towel bundles, or easing eager hands into terra-cotta pots. Good things are hidden inside that can be nibbled upon for the satisfaction of the soul.

Take *samosas*, for instance, those triangular, savory pastries. The best place to eat them is right on the street, when the odors wafting from a nearby *samosa* maker become too overwhelming to resist. All kinds of kebabs, marinated and grilled meat cubes, are also sold at open stalls. This is done deliberately to entice passing strollers.

All workers in India stop for tea, a custom not too different from the British one. But what is served, is a bit different. There would be tea, of course, perhaps *masala chai* ("spiced tea"; see page 234) or coffee. Then, an odd assortment might appear – *samosas*, fried cashews, and, to sweeten the mouth, some carrot *halva* (see page 230)!

In this chapter, there are also snacks that may be served with drinks, such as cocktail *koftas* (meatballs) that lend themselves very well to having toothpicks stuck in them, and spicy potato matchsticks.

I have included some soups in this chapter as well. Even though we do not, as a nation, drink soups, most Westernized Indians have happily adapted soups from other nations to suit their own tastes.

soups, snacks, and savories

chicken mulligatawny soup

There are many soupy dishes in India that are served with rice. It was probably one of these that inspired Anglo-Indian communities three centuries ago to create a soup that had Indian spices and ingredients in it, yet could be served at the start of a meal. There are hundreds of recipes for mulligatawny soup in India, all slightly different. For this book, I have chosen one in which the base is a purée of red split lentils (*masoor dal*). It is a hearty soup that can almost be a meal in itself. It is traditional to have some plain boiled rice with this soup. I usually serve it on the side, in small quantities.

Serves 4 to 6

175 g (1 cup) red split lentils (*moong dal*), picked over, washed, and drained

1.2 liters (5 cups) chicken stock

1/2 teaspoon ground turmeric

1 medium potato

5 cloves garlic, peeled

3 cm (1 1/4 inch) cube fresh ginger, peeled and coarsely grated

About 275 ml (1 1/4 cups) water

1 chicken breast, boned and skinned, with a net weight of about 200 g (7 oz)

1 1/4 teaspoons salt

Freshly ground black pepper

3 tablespoons vegetable oil

1 teaspoon ground cumin

1 teaspoon ground coriander

1/8 –1/4 teaspoon cayenne pepper

About 1 tablespoon lemon juice (you might want more)

Combine the lentils, chicken stock, and turmeric in a heavy, medium-sized pot and bring to a boil. Cover, leaving the lid just very slightly ajar, turn heat to low, and simmer gently for 30 minutes.

While the soup simmers, peel the potato and cut into 1 cm (1/2 inch) dice. When the soup has cooked for 30 minutes, add the potato dice to it. Cover, leaving the lid slightly ajar again, and continue the simmering for another 30 minutes.

During this second simmering period, put the garlic and ginger into the container of an electric blender. Add 4 1/2 tablespoons water and blend until you have a smooth paste.

Remove all fat from the chicken breast and cut it into 1 cm (1/2 inch) dice. Put the chicken in a bowl. Sprinkle 1/4 teaspoon of the salt and some black pepper over it. Toss to mix.

Once the soup base has finished cooking, it needs to be puréed. I do this in a blender, in three batches. Put the puréed soup in a bowl. Add the remaining 1 teaspoon salt and mix.

Rinse and wipe out your soup pot. Pour the oil into it and set it over medium heat. When the oil is hot, put in the garlic-ginger paste, the cumin, coriander, and cayenne. Fry, stirring continuously, until the spice mixture is slightly browned and separates from the oil. Put in the chicken pieces. Stir and fry another 2–3 minutes or until the chicken pieces turn quite opaque. Add 250 ml (1 cup) water and bring to a boil. Cover, turn heat to low, and simmer for 3 minutes or until chicken is cooked. Pour in the puréed soup and the lemon juice. Stir to mix and bring to a simmer. Taste the soup for seasonings. I usually add another teaspoon or so of lemon juice. Simmer the soup very gently for another 2 minutes. If it is too thick, you can always thin it out with a little chicken stock or water.

green soup

Hara shorva

This is India's version of cream of pea soup. It is delicate and quite delicious.

Serves 5 to 6

1 medium potato, peeled and roughly diced

1 medium onion, peeled and coarsely chopped

1.2 liters (5 cups) chicken stock

2 cm (3/4 inch) cube fresh ginger, peeled

1/2 teaspoon ground coriander

2 teaspoons ground cumin

5 tablespoons chopped cilantro

1/2 fresh, hot green chili

275 g (10 oz) shelled peas, fresh or frozen

3/4 teaspoon salt (more if the stock is unsalted)

1 tablespoon lemon juice

1/2 teaspoon ground, roasted cumin seeds (page 20)

150 ml (2/3 cup) heavy cream

Combine the potato, onion, chicken stock, ginger, ground coriander, and ground cumin in a pot and bring to a boil. Cover, turn heat to low, and simmer for 30 minutes. Fish out the cube of ginger and discard it. Add the cilantro, green chili, peas, salt, lemon juice, and ground, roasted cumin seeds. Bring to a boil and simmer, uncovered, for 2–3 minutes or until the peas are just tender. Empty the soup into the container of an electric blender in 2 or 3 batches and blend until it is smooth. Put the soup into a clean pot. Add the cream and bring to a simmer to heat through.

cold yogurt soup
with mint

Dahi ka shorva

Nothing could be more pleasant in the summer than this soothing, cooling soup that probably originated in the Caucasus and then came down to India with wandering Turks, Persians, and Moguls.

Serves 4 to 6

570 ml (2 2/3 cups) plain yogurt

275 ml (1 1/4 cups) light cream

425 ml (2 cups) cold, defatted chicken stock

1/2 teaspoon ground, roasted cumin seeds (page 20)

1/2 teaspoon salt (more if the stock is unsalted)

Freshly ground black pepper

2 teaspoons lemon juice

1 tablespoon very, very finely chopped, fresh mint or 1 teaspoon dried mint flakes, crumbled into a powder

Put the yogurt into a bowl. Beat lightly with a fork or a whisk until smooth and creamy. Pour in the cream. Beat gently to mix. Add the chicken stock, ground, roasted cumin seeds, salt, black pepper, lemon juice, and mint. Stir to mix and taste for seasoning.

skewered chicken kebabs

Murghi tikka

You could serve these pieces of marinated and baked chicken as a first course or you could cut them in halves, stick toothpicks in them, and pass them around with drinks. This dish belongs to the same family as Tandoori chicken and should, ideally, be cooked in a *tandoor* or clay oven. I find that home ovens, heated to their maximum temperature, make adequate substitutes.

Murghi tikka is a useful dish to have in one's repertoire. Most of the work — and it is not that much — can be done a day ahead of time. All that remains then is to brush the chicken pieces with butter and slip them into the oven for about 15 minutes.

Serves 4 to 6

3 chicken breasts, boned and skinned (net weight after boning and skinning about 1.25 kg/2¾ lb)

1¼ teaspoons salt

1 juicy lemon

6 tablespoons plain yogurt

2.5 cm (1 inch) cube fresh ginger, peeled and finely grated

3 cloves garlic, peeled and mashed to a pulp

1 teaspoon ground cumin

⅛–¼ teaspoon cayenne pepper

¼ teaspoon *garam masala* (page 21)

2 teaspoons yellow liquid food coloring mixed with ½ teaspoon red liquid food coloring

About 115 g (½ cup) unsalted butter, melted

Remove all the fat from the chicken pieces. Cut each breast in half, lengthwise, and then cut each half, crosswise, into 3 or 4 more or less equal pieces. Lay the pieces in a single layer on a plate. Sprinkle half the salt over them. Squeeze the juice from half the lemon over them as well. Rub the salt and lemon into the chicken. Turn the chicken pieces over and do the same on the second side with the remaining salt and lemon half. Set aside for 20 minutes.

Meanwhile, put the yogurt in a small bowl. Beat it with a fork or whisk until it is smooth and creamy. Add the ginger, garlic, cumin, cayenne, and *garam masala*. Stir to mix.

After the chicken has sat around in its first marinade for 20 minutes, brush one side with the food coloring. Turn the chicken pieces over with a pair of tongs and brush the second side with the coloring. Put the chicken pieces and all accumulated juices in a bowl. Hold a strainer over the chicken pieces. Pour the yogurt mixture into the strainer and then push through as much of it as you can with a rubber spatula. Fold this second marinade over the chicken pieces. Cover tightly and refrigerate for 6–24 hours.

Preheat your oven to its maximum temperature and place a shelf in its top section.

Thread the chicken pieces on skewers, leaving a little space between each piece. Balance the skewers on the raised rim of a baking pan, making sure that the meat juices will drip on to the pan and not your oven floor. Brush the chicken with half the melted butter and put in the oven for about 7 minutes. Take out the baking pan and skewers. Turn the chicken pieces over and brush again with butter. Bake another 8–10 minutes or until the chicken is just done. Do not overcook.

baked lamb shami kebabs

Ovan ke shami kebab

Traditionally, *shami kebabs*, which are spicy, hamburgerlike patties made with finely minced lamb, are sautéed in a frying pan. Once, in order to cut down on the use of oil, I tried baking them instead. The result was excellent and I am reproducing it here for you. You can serve these kebabs, cut into squares, with drinks or as part of a meal.

Serves 4 to 8

1 medium onion peeled and cut into paper-thin rings plus 1 medium onion peeled and finely chopped

2–3 fresh, hot green chilies, finely chopped

5 tablespoons finely chopped, fresh mint

Salt

1½ tablespoons lemon juice

4 tablespoons blanched, slivered almonds

2 tablespoons white poppy seeds

450 g (1 lb) twice-ground lamb (it should be very fine)

1 teaspoon ground cumin

1 teaspoon *garam masala* (page 21)

¼ teaspoon cayenne pepper

3 tablespoons plain yogurt

A little unsalted butter

Sprigs of mint, to garnish

Put the onion rings into a bowl. Add icy water to cover. Cover the bowl with cling film and refrigerate until needed (1–5 hours).

Put the chopped onion into a bowl. Add the green chilies, mint, ¼ teaspoon salt, and the lemon juice. Stir to mix and set aside for 20 minutes or longer.

Set a small cast-iron frying pan over medium-high heat. When very hot, put in the almonds. Stir, shake, or toss the almonds until they are roasted and turn golden. Remove to a plate and allow to cool a bit.

Put the poppy seeds into the same hot frying pan. Stir and roast for a minute or two or until they emit a roasted aroma and turn a shade darker. Remove to a separate plate and allow to cool a bit.

Put the almonds into the container of a clean coffee grinder or other spice grinder and grind as finely as possible. Put into a large bowl. Put the poppy seeds into the same grinder and grind as finely as possible. Empty into the same large bowl. Also put into the large bowl the lamb, ground cumin, *garam masala*, cayenne, yogurt, 1 teaspoon salt, and the onion-mint-chili mixture with all its accumulated juices. Mix well, almost kneading to incorporate all the ingredients. Form into a rough ball.

Preheat the oven to 180°C/350°F.

Rub a 5 cm (2 inch) deep 20 x 20 cm (8 x 8 inch) nonstick baking pan lightly with butter. Put the ball of meat in its center. Using your fingers, pat the ball down, easing it evenly toward the edges of the square pan. You will now have a very large, flat, square "kebab." It should be evenly flat at the top.

Bake for 50 minutes. Remove. Pour out all the accumulated liquid. Heat the grill. When it is very hot, put the baking pan under it briefly – for about a minute – until the meat browns lightly on the top.

To serve: Cut the meat into 2.5 cm (1 inch) squares and arrange on a plate. Garnish with the sprigs of mint. Drain the soaking onions in a strainer and empty into the center of a dish towel. Bring the edges of the dish towel together and twist the area where the onions are, to squeeze out as much of the moisture as possible. Spread the onions over the kebabs and serve.

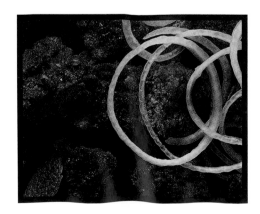

lamb or beef kebabs

Boti kabab

These kebabs make excellent nibbling fare for snacks.

Serves 4 as a snack

225–250 g (8–9 oz) boned lamb from shoulder or leg, or beef steak

4 tablespoons plain yogurt

1½ tablespoons lemon juice

2.5 cm (1 inch) cube fresh ginger, peeled and very finely grated

1 clove garlic, peeled and mashed to a pulp

1 teaspoon ground cumin

½ teaspoon ground coriander

¼ teaspoon cayenne pepper

¾ teaspoon salt

1½ tablespoons vegetable oil

Cut the meat into 2 cm (¾ inch) cubes and put in a stainless-steel or other non-metallic bowl.

Combine the yogurt, lemon juice, ginger, garlic, cumin, coriander, cayenne, and salt in a bowl and mix well with a fork. Hold a strainer over the meat and pour the yogurt mixture into it. Push this mixture through the strainer, extracting all the paste that you can. Mix the meat and the marinade well. Cover and refrigerate for 6–24 hours.

Heat your grill.

Thread the meat onto skewers. Balance the skewers on the edge of a baking pan in such a way that all the meat juices drip inside the pan. Brush the kebabs generously with oil and place the baking pan under the grill. When one side of the meat gets lightly browned, turn the skewers to brown the opposite side, making sure to brush this side first with more oil.

delicious cocktail koftas

Chhote kofte

Almost every country has some type of meatball. This Indian one is made out of minced lamb and you can eat it as part of a meal or you could stick toothpicks into the *koftas* and serve them as snacks.

Makes 30 meatballs and serves 6 for snacks, 4 for dinner

FOR THE MEATBALLS

450 g (1 lb) ground lamb

1/2 teaspoon salt

1 teaspoon ground cumin

1 teaspoon ground coriander

1/4 teaspoon *garam masala* (page 21)

1/8 teaspoon cayenne pepper

2 tablespoons very finely chopped cilantro

3 tablespoons plain yogurt

FOR THE SAUCE

5 cloves garlic, peeled

2.5 cm (1 inch) cube fresh ginger, peeled and coarsely chopped

335 ml (1 1/2 cups) water

1 teaspoon ground cumin

1 teaspoon ground coriander

1 teaspoon bright red paprika

1/4 teaspoon cayenne pepper

5 tablespoons vegetable oil

2.5 cm (1 inch) cinnamon stick

6 cardamom pods

6 cloves

1 large onion, peeled and finely chopped

1 medium tomato, peeled (page 30) and chopped (a small can of tomatoes may be substituted)

4 tablespoons plain yogurt

1/2 teaspoon salt

To make the meatballs: Combine all the ingredients for the meatballs. Dip your hands in water whenever you need to and form about 30 meatballs.

For the sauce, put the garlic and ginger into the container of a food processor or blender along with 4 tablespoons water. Blend until you have a paste. Put the paste in a bowl. Add the cumin, coriander, paprika, and cayenne. Stir to mix.

To make the sauce: Put the oil in a heavy, 23–25 cm (9–10 inch) wide pan or frying pan and set over medium-high heat. When hot, put in the cinnamon, cardamom pods, and cloves. Stir them for 3–4 seconds. Now put in the chopped onions and fry them, stirring all the time, until they are reddish brown in color. Turn the heat to medium and put in the paste from the bowl as well as the chopped tomatoes. Stir and fry this mixture until it turns a brownish color. When it begins to brown, add 1 tablespoon of the yogurt. Stir and fry some more until the yogurt is incorporated into the sauce. Now add another tablespoon of yogurt. Incorporate that into the sauce as well. Keep doing this until you have put in all the yogurt. Now put in 275 ml (1 1/4 cups) water and the salt. Stir and bring to a simmer.

Put in all the meatballs in a single layer. Cover, leaving the lid very slightly ajar, turn heat to low, and cook for 25 minutes. Stir very gently every 5 minutes or so, making sure not to break the meatballs. Toward the end of the cooking period, you should scrape the bottom of the pan just to make sure the sauce is not burning. If necessary, add a tablespoon or so of water. Remove the lid and turn the heat up to medium-low. Stir gently and cook until the meatballs have a browned look. All the sauce should now be clinging to the meatballs and there should be just a little fat left at the bottom of the pan.

When you are ready to eat, heat the *koftas* gently. Lift them out of the fat and shake off any whole spices that may be clinging to them. Stick a toothpick into each *kofta* if serving with drinks.

If you have these *koftas* for dinner, you could leave more of a sauce.

tandoori-style shrimp

These marinated shrimp are traditionally cooked in a *tandoor*. I cook them very quickly in a frying pan. You may easily double the recipe, if you wish to serve these shrimp as a main course. Just use a larger frying pan.

Serves 4 as a snack

4 tablespoons plain yogurt

2.5 cm (1 inch) cube fresh ginger, peeled and very finely grated

1 large clove garlic, peeled and mashed to a pulp

5 teaspoons lemon juice

$1/4$ teaspoon salt, or to taste

Freshly ground black pepper

$1^1/2$ teaspoons ground, roasted cumin seeds (page 20)

$1/4$ teaspoon *garam masala* (page 21)

2 teaspoons yellow liquid food coloring mixed with 1 teaspoon red liquid food coloring

335 g ($3/4$ pound) peeled good-quality frozen shrimp, defrosted and patted dry

50 g (4 tablespoons) unsalted butter

Put the yogurt in a bowl. Beat lightly with a fork or a whisk until it is smooth and creamy. Add the ginger, garlic, lemon juice, salt, some black pepper, ground, roasted cumin seeds, *garam masala,* and liquid food coloring. Stir to mix and set aside for 15 minutes. Push this liquid through a strainer into a second bowl. Add the shrimp to the marinade and mix well. Set aside for 30 minutes. Remove the shrimp with a slotted spoon, leaving all the marinade behind in the bowl.

Melt the butter in a 20–23 cm (8–9 inch) frying pan over medium heat. When the butter has melted completely, turn heat to medium high and immediately pour in the marinade. Stir and fry for a few minutes or until the butter separates and you have a thick bubbly sauce clinging to the bottom of the pan. Add the shrimp and fold them in. Cook for a few minutes, stirring gently. Do not overcook the shrimp.

Serve immediately.

quick-fried shrimp

You may stick toothpicks in these shrimp and pass them around with drinks or serve them as a main course.

Serves 4 to 6

75 g ($^3/_4$ cup) rice flour (cornflour may be substituted)

2 teaspoons ground turmeric

1 tablespoon cayenne pepper

2 tablespoons ground cumin

2$^1/_2$ teaspoons salt

About 1 teaspoon freshly ground black pepper

Vegetable oil for deep-frying

450 g (1 lb) peeled, good-quality frozen shrimp, defrosted and patted dry

1 lemon, halved

Mix together the flour, turmeric, cayenne, cumin, salt, and black pepper. Put about 4 cm (1½ inches) oil to heat in a deep frying pan, or other utensil for deep-frying over medium heat. Meanwhile, dip the shrimp in the flour mixture and coat them thoroughly. When the oil is hot, put in as many shrimp as the utensil will hold in a single layer. Fry until the shrimp turn slightly crisp on the outside – just a minute or so – turning them whenever you need to. Remove with a slotted spoon and drain on a paper towel. Do as many batches of shrimp as you need to and serve them hot, with a little lemon juice squeezed over them.

Note: This is quite a "fiery" dish. If you don't like your food too "hot," you should substantially reduce the amount of cayenne pepper!

spicy matchstick potato crisps

Aloo ka tala hua laccha

This is one of those snack foods that Indians munch noisily while watching Indian movie epics in which bandits chase weeping, but upstanding, heroines and scantily clad girls shake their hips at the dashing heroes.

Serves 4 to 6 with drinks

1 medium onion, peeled and coarsely chopped

2–3 cloves garlic, peeled

1 dried, hot red chili
(use more if you want the potatoes to be more than mildly hot)

1 teaspoon ground cumin

$\frac{1}{2}$ teaspoon ground coriander

4 medium potatoes

Enough vegetable oil to have 1 cm ($\frac{1}{2}$ inch) in a big frying pan

$\frac{3}{4}$–1 teaspoon salt

Put the onion, garlic, and red chili into the container of an electric blender or food processor. Blend until you have a paste, pushing down with a rubber spatula if necessary. Empty the paste into a bowl. Add the cumin and coriander and mix them in.

Peel the potatoes and cut them into 3 mm ($\frac{1}{8}$ inch) thick slices. You may use a mandolin, food processor, or knife to do this. Stack about 5 slices together at a time and cut them into 3 mm ($\frac{1}{8}$ inch) wide matchsticks. (You can either fry the potatoes as soon as they are cut or else leave them to soak in water and pat them dry.)

Line one very large or two smaller plates with paper towels and place near the stove.

Put about 1 cm ($\frac{1}{2}$ inch) oil in a deep, 25–30 cm (10–12 inch) frying pan and set over medium heat. When hot, put in as many of the cut potatoes as the pan will hold easily without overcrowding. Stir and fry until the potatoes are golden and crisp. Remove the potatoes with a slotted spoon and spread them out on one area of the platter. Fry all the potatoes this way, spreading out each batch on the paper towels.

Take the frying pan off the heat and remove all but 4 tablespoons of the oil. Put the frying pan back on the medium heat and pour in the spice mixture from the bowl. Stir and fry it until it is brown and fairly dry. Take your time to do this, turning the heat down a bit if you think it is necessary. Now put in all the fried potatoes and the salt. Stir to mix, breaking up spice lumps as you do so. Drain again and serve.

poppadums

Paapar

These thin, crisp disks are sold in markets either plain or flavored with spices and seasonings such as garlic or black pepper or red pepper. They are partially prepared. A seasoned dough made from dried pulses has already been rolled out into the required shapes and then dried in the sun. All that you have to do is cook the poppadum. The cooking process is quick and easy.

There are two basic methods to choose from. Deep-frying is the traditional method. This allows the poppadums to expand to their fullest and turn very airy. It also brings out their full flavor. This method does, however, leave those who are nibbling the poppadum with slightly greasy fingers. The second method is to roast the poppadums directly over or under heat. This way you end up with clean fingers and poppadums with fewer calories. But the poppadums do not expand as much and remain denser than fried ones. Poppadums may be served with drinks or with Indian meals of any sort.

Serves 6

6 poppadums

Vegetable oil for deep-frying

THE FRYING METHOD:

Depending upon the size of the poppadums, either leave them whole or snap each into 2 halves. Remember that they will expand in the frying pan.

Put about 2 cm (¾ inch) oil in a frying pan and set over medium heat. When hot, put in a poppadum (or half a poppadum, depending upon the size of the frying pan and poppadum). It will sizzle and expand within seconds. Remove the poppadum with a slotted spoon and drain on paper towels. Cook all poppadums this way.

Poppadums should retain their yellowish color and not turn brown. They should also cook very fast, so you may find it necessary to adjust your heat.

Serves 6

6 poppadums

THE ROASTING METHOD:

Heat your grill. Put 1 poppadum on a rack and place it about 5–7.5 cm (2–3 inches) under the grill. Now watch it very carefully. It will expand in seconds. It will also turn paler and develop a few bubbles. Turn it over and expose the second side to the heat for a second or so. Watch it all the time and do not let it brown or burn. Remove from the grill. Make all poppadums this way. (When making poppadums under a grill, it is not always necessary to turn them over. You will have to use your own judgment here.)

Poppadums may also be roasted directly on top of a live flame. Of course, you can only do this if you have a gas stove. If you wish to follow this method, turn the flame on low. Now grip a poppadum with a set of tongs and hold it half an inch above the flame. The part of the poppadum that is directly over the flame will bubble and turn lighter in color. When that happens, expose another part of the poppadum to the flame.

Keep doing this until the entire poppadum has been roasted.

fried cashews

Tale huay caju

Cashews that have been freshly fried at home have an exquisite taste, far better than that of the bought variety. In India, this was the only kind of cashew we ate, with my mother frying the nuts just before my father sat down for his evening Scotch and soda.

Serves 4 to 6

Vegetable oil for deep-frying
225 g (2 cups) raw cashew nuts
1/4 teaspoon salt
Freshly ground black pepper

Put a strainer on top of a metal bowl and set it near the stove. Also, line 2 plates with paper towels and put them nearby.

Put about 2.5 cm (1 inch) oil in a deep, 20 cm (8 inch) frying pan and place over medium heat. When hot, put in all the cashews. Stir and fry them until they turn a reddish gold color. This happens fairly fast. Now empty the contents of the frying pan into the strainer to drain the oil. Lift up the strainer and shake out all the extra oil. Spread the cashews out on one of the plates and sprinkle the salt and black pepper on them. Stir to mix. Now slide the cashews onto the second plate. This will take some more of the oil off them. Serve cashews warm or after they have cooled off.

deep-fried, stuffed savory pastry

Samosa

Samosas make excellent appetizers. If you wish to use a minced meat stuffing, use the recipe for Minced Lamb with Mint (page 59). Boil away the liquid and drain the fat. Stuff each *samosa* with about 2½ tablespoons of the cooked mince. *Samosas* are delicious with Cilantro Chutney (page 218). Here is my recipe for *samosas* with a potato stuffing.

Makes 16 samosas

FOR THE PASTRY

225 g (2 cups) plain flour

½ teaspoon salt

4 tablespoons vegetable oil plus a bit more

4 tablespoons water

FOR THE STUFFING

4–5 medium potatoes, boiled in their jackets and allowed to cool

4 tablespoons vegetable oil

1 medium-sized onion, peeled and finely chopped

175 g (1 cup) shelled peas, fresh or frozen (if frozen, defrost them first)

1 tablespoon peeled, finely grated fresh ginger

1 fresh, hot green chili, finely chopped

3 tablespoons very finely chopped cilantro

About 3 tablespoons water

1½ teaspoons salt, or to taste

1 teaspoon ground coriander

1 teaspoon *garam masala* (page 21)

1 teaspoon ground, roasted cumin seeds (page 20)

¼ teaspoon cayenne pepper

2 tablespoons lemon juice

Vegetable oil for deep-frying

Sift the flour and salt into a bowl. Add the 4 tablespoons of vegetable oil and rub it in with your fingers until the mixture resembles coarse breadcrumbs. Slowly add about 4 tablespoons water – or a tiny bit more – and form the dough into a stiff ball.

Empty the ball out onto a clean work surface. Knead the dough for about 10 minutes or until it is smooth. Make a ball. Rub the ball with about ¼ teaspoon oil and slip it into a plastic bag. Set it aside for 30 minutes or longer.

Make the stuffing: Peel the potatoes and cut them into 5 mm (¼ inch) dice. Put 4 tablespoons oil in a large frying pan and place over medium heat. When hot, put in the onions. Stir and fry them until they begin to turn brown at the edges. Add the peas, ginger, green chili, cilantro, and 3 tablespoons water. Cover, lower heat, and simmer until the peas are cooked. Stir every now and then and add a little more water if the frying pan seems to dry out.

Add the diced potatoes, salt, ground coriander, *garam masala*, ground, roasted cumin seeds, cayenne, and lemon juice. Stir to mix. Cook on low heat for 3–4 minutes, stirring gently as you do so. Check balance of salt and lemon juice. You may want more of both. Turn off the heat and allow the mixture to cool.

Knead the pastry dough again and divide it into 8 balls. Keep 7 covered while you work with the eighth. Roll this ball out into a 18 cm (7 inch) round. Cut it into half with a sharp, pointed knife. Pick up one half and form a cone, making a 5 mm (¼ inch) wide overlapping seam. Glue this seam together with a little water. Fill the cone with about 2½ tablespoons of the potato mixture. Close the top of the cone by sticking the open edges together with a little water.

Again, your seam should be about 5 mm (¼ inch) wide. Press the top seam down with the prongs of a fork or flute it with your fingers. Make 15 more *samosas*.

Put about 4–5 cm (1½–2 inches) oil in a small, deep frying pan or Indian *karhai* and set over medium-low heat. When the oil is medium-hot, put in as many *samosas* as the pan will hold in single layer. Fry slowly, turning the *samosas* frequently until they are golden brown and crisp. Drain on paper towels and serve hot, warm, or at room temperature.

This chapter has a great variety of meat dishes in it, going from *Kheema matar* (Minced Meat with Peas) and *Chhole wala gosht* (Pork Chops with Chick Peas) that you may wish to cook for your family, to *Raan masaledar* – a whole leg of lamb garnished with almonds and raisins – which would impress the most blasé of guests.

There are a lot of lamb recipes. We do eat a fair amount of lamb in India. We also eat a lot of goat. As goat is hard to find in the West, I have substituted lamb in its place. I find that the best cuts of lamb for stewing come from the neck and shoulder. You should buy a whole shoulder and carve up the meat yourself. Or you could buy shoulder chops and cut them up with a heavy cleaver. There is a lot of connective tissue in the shoulder and neck. This eventually makes for a moister meat.

In India, we usually leave the bone in the meat when we are cooking any stew-type dish. In fact, we throw in a few extra marrow bones for good measure because they affect the taste and texture of the sauce. However, many recipes in this book call for boned lamb. This is only because, over the years, I have seen many guests struggle with bones and have come to the conclusion that just because I like bones (I suck them), there is no reason to inflict them upon my guests. A majority of people who dine in our house seem to prefer boned meat. I leave the bone-in or bone-out decision up to you. Just remember that bones in stewing meat such as shoulder make up about 40 percent of the total volume. If my recipe is for boned meat and you decide to leave the bone in, you might feed just half the number of people.

In India, we frequently cook meat with vegetables such as potatoes and turnips. They absorb its taste and lend their own flavor to the sauce.

I have included a few recipes for beef and pork as many communities in India eat them. I, for one, simply love the Beef Baked with Yogurt and Black Pepper as well as the spicy and sour pork *vindaloo*, a Goan speciality.

meat

minced lamb with mint

Pudine wala kheema

This dish may be served with rice, a pulse (such as Whole Green Lentils with Spinach and Ginger, page 168), and a yogurt relish. I often use it to stuff tomatoes. Get firm, good-sized tomatoes and slice off a cap at the top. Scoop out the inside without breaking the skin and then season the inside of the tomato with salt and pepper. Stuff loosely with the mince, put the caps back on, and bake in a 200°C/400°F oven for 15 minutes or until the skin begins to crinkle. Serve with rice and a salad.

Serves 6

2 medium onions, peeled

8–9 cloves garlic, peeled

5 x 2.5 cm (2 x 1 inch) piece fresh ginger, peeled and coarsely chopped

3 tablespoons water

2 tablespoons ground cumin

4 teaspoons ground coriander

1 teaspoon ground turmeric

1/4 –1 teaspoon cayenne pepper

4 tablespoons vegetable oil

4 cardamom pods

6 cloves

900 g (2 lb) minced lamb

About 1 1/2 teaspoons salt

50 g (1 cup) finely chopped, fresh mint

1/4 teaspoon *garam masala* (page 21)

1 1/2 tablespoons lemon juice

Chop half the onions finely and set aside. Chop the other half coarsely and put them, along with the garlic, ginger, and water into the container of an electric blender. Blend to a smooth paste. Empty into a small bowl. Add the cumin, coriander, turmeric, and cayenne. Mix.

Put the oil in a 25 cm (10 inch) frying pan and place over high heat. When hot, put in the cardamom pods and cloves. Two seconds later, put in the finely chopped onions. Stir and fry them until they turn fairly brown. Turn the heat to medium and put in the spice mixture. Stir and fry for 3–4 minutes. If the spice mixture sticks to the pan, sprinkle in a tablespoon of water and keep frying.

Put in the minced meat. Break up all the lumps and stir the mince until it loses all its pinkness. Stir and fry another minute after that. Add the salt and mix. Cover, turn heat to very low, and let the mince cook in its own juices for 25 minutes. Remove the cover and spoon off most of the accumulated fat. Add the chopped mint, *garam masala,* and lemon juice. Stir to mix and bring to a simmer. Cover, and simmer on very low heat for 3 minutes.

Note: The cardamom pods and cloves are not meant to be eaten.

kashmiri meatballs

Kashmiri koftas

These sausage-shaped "meatballs" taste very Kashmiri in their final blend of flavors.
I often serve them with Plain Basmati Rice (page 193), Red Split Lentils with Cumin
Seeds (page 165), and Carrot and Onion Salad (page 217).

Serves 6

900 g (2 lb) ground lamb
Piece of fresh ginger, about 4 cm
(1½ inches) long and 2.5 cm
(1 inch) thick, peeled, and finely grated
1 tablespoon ground cumin
1 tablespoon ground coriander
¼ teaspoon ground cloves
¼ teaspoon ground cinnamon
⅛ teaspoon grated nutmeg
¼ teaspoon freshly ground black pepper
⅛ –¼ teaspoon cayenne pepper
About 1¼ teaspoons salt
5 tablespoons plain yogurt
7–8 tablespoons vegetable oil
5 cm (2 inch) cinnamon stick
5–6 cardamom pods
2 bay leaves
5–6 cloves
225 ml (1 cup) warm water

Combine the lamb, ginger, cumin, coriander, ground cloves, ground cinnamon, grated nutmeg, black pepper, cayenne, salt, and 3 tablespoons of the yogurt in a bowl. Mix well.

Wet your hands with cold water and form 24 long *koftas* – sausage shapes, about 6–7.5 cm (2½–3 inches) long and about 2.5 cm (1 inch) thick.

Heat the oil in a large, preferably nonstick, frying pan (or use two frying pans). When hot, put in the cinnamon stick, cardamom pods, bay leaves, and cloves. Stir for a second. Now put in the *koftas* in a single layer and fry them on medium-high heat until they are lightly browned on all sides. Beat the remaining yogurt into the 225 ml (1 cup) warm water. Pour this over the *koftas* and bring to a boil. Cover, lower heat, and simmer for about 30 minutes, turning the *koftas* gently every 7–8 minutes. By the end of the 30 minutes no liquid other than the fat should be left in the frying pan. If necessary, turn up the heat to achieve this.

When you get ready to serve, lift the *koftas* out of the fat with a slotted spoon. Leave the whole spices behind as well – they are not meant to be eaten.

minced meat with peas

Kheema matar

I associate this dish with very pleasurable family picnics that we had, sometimes in the private compartments of slightly sooty, steam-engined trains, and sometimes in the immaculate public gardens of historic Mogul palaces. The mince, invariably at room temperature, was eaten with *pooris* or *parathas* that had been stacked tightly in aluminium containers. There was always a pickle, to perk things up, and some kind of onion relish as well.

Serves 4 to 6

4 tablespoons vegetable oil

1 medium onion, peeled and finely chopped

6–7 medium-sized cloves garlic, peeled and finely chopped

700 g (1^1/$_2$ lb) minced lamb (minced beef may be substituted)

2.5 cm (1 inch) cube fresh ginger, peeled and grated to a pulp

1–2 fresh, hot green chilies, minced

1 teaspoon ground coriander

1 teaspoon ground cumin

^{1}/$_8$ –^{1}/$_4$ teaspoon cayenne pepper

275 ml (1^1/$_4$ cups) water

285 g (1^1/$_2$ cups) shelled peas

4–6 heaped tablespoons chopped cilantro

About 1^1/$_4$ teaspoons salt

1 teaspoon *garam masala* (page 21)

About 1^1/$_2$ tablespoons lemon juice

Put the oil in a wide, medium-sized pot and place over medium-high heat. When hot, put in the chopped onions. Stir and fry them until they are lightly browned. Add the garlic. Stir and fry for another minute. Now put in the mince, ginger, green chilies, ground coriander, cumin, and cayenne. Stir and fry the meat for 5 minutes, breaking up lumps as you do so. Add 175 ml (^{3}/$_4$ cup) of the water and bring to a boil. Cover, turn heat to low, and simmer for 30 minutes.

Add the peas, cilantro, salt, *garam masala*, lemon juice, and the remaining water. Mix and bring to a simmer. Cover and cook on low heat another 10 minutes or until the peas are tender. Taste seasonings and adjust the balance of salt and lemon juice if you need to.

A lot of fat might have collected at the bottom of your pot. Whenever you get ready to serve, lift the mince and peas out of the fat with a slotted spoon. Do not serve the fat.

kashmiri lamb stew

Kashmiri yakhni

This is really a lamb stew – with lots of lovely fennel flavor but no hot chilies – that is thickened with yogurt so it has a creamy tartness. You could serve it with plain rice, as Kashmiris do.

Serves 4 to 6

4 teaspoons fennel seeds

6 tablespoons vegetable oil or *ghee*

Pinch of ground asafetida (optional)

1 kg 350 g (3 lb) shoulder of lamb, boned or unboned, cut roughly into 5 cm (2 inch) cubes

2.5 cm (1 inch) cinnamon stick

10 cardamom pods

15 cloves

1¾ teaspoons salt, or to taste

885 ml (3¾ cups) water

1½ teaspoons dried ginger powder

425 ml (1¾ cups) plain yogurt

¼ teaspoon *garam masala* (page 21)

Put the fennel seeds into a clean coffee grinder or other spice grinder and grind to a powder.

Put the oil or *ghee* in a heavy, wide pot and place over high heat. When hot, put in the asafetida, if using. One second later, put in all the meat, as well as the cinnamon, cardamom pods, cloves, and salt. Stir and cook, uncovered, over high heat for about 5 minutes or until almost all the water released by the meat disappears and the meat browns very lightly. Lower the heat to medium and add 1 tablespoon water, the fennel, and ginger. Stir to mix. Add 845 ml (3⅔ cups) water, cover partially, and simmer on medium heat for 30 minutes.

Cover completely, turn heat to low, and simmer for 40 minutes or until the meat is tender. Stir a few times as the meat cooks, adding a few tablespoons of water if it dries out.

Beat the yogurt in a bowl until it is smooth and creamy.

Remove the cover from the meat pot and turn the heat to medium-low. Push the meat cubes to the edges of the pan, leaving a well-like space in the center. Pour the yogurt very slowly into this well, while moving a slotted spoon back and forth quite fast in the same area. (If you do not do this, the yogurt will curdle.) Keep up the back-and-forth movement of the slotted spoon for a good 5 minutes *after* all the yogurt has been poured in. You should now have a simmering, creamy sauce. Cover partially and cook on medium-low heat for 10 minutes. Sprinkle in the *garam masala* and mix.

Note: The whole spices in the stew are not meant to be eaten.

lamb with onions

Do piaza

This is an elegant dish that may be made as mild or as hot as you like. It is cooked with a fair amount of oil but most of this is skimmed off the top before serving. There are some whole spices in it – cloves, cardamom, and cinnamon – which are not meant to be eaten. They should be pushed to the side as and when you come across them on your plates.

Lamb with Onions may be served with rice or a bread. Spicy Green Beans (page 132) also go well with it.

Serves 6

4 good-sized onions, peeled

7 cloves garlic, peeled

2.5 cm (1 inch) cube fresh ginger, coarsely chopped

425 ml (2 cups) water

10 tablespoons vegetable oil

2.5 cm (1 inch) cinnamon stick

10 cardamom pods

10 cloves

1 kg 125 g (2½ lb) boned lamb, preferably from the shoulder, cut into 2.5 cm (1 inch) cubes (with most of the fat removed)

1 tablespoon ground coriander

2 teaspoons ground cumin

6 tablespoons plain yogurt, beaten lightly

¼ –½ teaspoon cayenne pepper

About 1¼ teaspoons salt

½ teaspoon *garam masala* (page 21)

Cut three of the onions into halves, lengthwise, and then cut them, crosswise, into very fine rings. Chop the fourth onion finely. Keep the two types of onion separate.

Put the garlic and ginger into the container of an electric blender or food processor. Add 100 ml (¼ cup) of the measured water and blend until fairly smooth.

Put the oil in a wide, heavy pot and place over medium-high heat. When hot, put in the finely sliced onions. Stir and fry for 10–12 minutes or until the onions turn a nice, reddish brown color. You may have to turn the heat down somewhat toward the end of this cooking period. Remove the onions with a slotted spoon and spread them on a plate lined with paper towels.

Put the cinnamon, cardamom pods, and cloves into the hot oil. Stir them for about 5 seconds over medium-high heat. Now put in 8–10 cubes of meat or as many as the pot will hold easily in a single, loosely packed layer. Brown the meat on one side. Turn it over and brown the reverse side. Remove the meat cubes with a slotted spoon and put them in a bowl. Brown all the meat this way, removing each batch as it gets done.

Put the chopped onion into the remaining oil in the pot. Stir and fry it on medium heat until the pieces turn brown at the edges. Add the garlic-ginger paste. Stir and fry it until all the water in it seems to boil away and you see the oil again. Turn the heat down a bit and add the coriander and cumin. Stir and fry for 30 seconds. Now add 1 tablespoon of the yogurt. Stir and fry until it is incorporated into the sauce. Add another tablespoon of yogurt. Stir and fry, incorporating this into the sauce as well. Add all the yogurt this way, a tablespoon at a time. Now put in all the meat and any accumulated juices in the meat bowl with the remaining water, the cayenne, and the salt. Stir to mix and bring to a simmer. Cover, turn heat to low, and cook for about 45 minutes or until the lamb is tender. Add the fried onions and the *garam masala*. Stir to mix.

Continue to cook, uncovered, for another 2–3 minutes, stirring gently as you do so. Turn off the heat and let the pot sit for a while. The fat will rise to the top. Remove it with a spoon.

Note: This dish may be prepared ahead of time and reheated.

lamb with spinach

Dilli ka saag gosht

This dish could also be made with beef. Use cubed chuck steak and cook it for about 2 hours or until it is tender. *Dilli ka saag gosht* may be served with rice or bread. I think Fried Eggplant Slices (page 134) and a yogurt dish would complement the meat well.

Serves 6

8 tablespoons vegetable oil

1/4 teaspoon black peppercorns

6–7 whole cloves

2 bay leaves

6 cardamom pods

2 medium onions, peeled and finely chopped

6–8 cloves garlic, peeled and finely chopped

2.5 cm (1 inch) cube fresh ginger, peeled and finely chopped

900 g (2 lb) boned lamb from the shoulder, cut into 2.5 cm (1 inch) cubes

2 teaspoons ground cumin

1 teaspoon ground coriander

1/4 –3/4 teaspoon cayenne pepper

2 teaspoons salt

5 tablespoons plain yogurt, well beaten

900 g (2 lb) fresh spinach, trimmed, washed and finely chopped; 900 g (2 lb) frozen spinach, thawed, may be substituted

1/4 teaspoon *garam masala* (page 21)

Put the oil in a large pot and place over medium-high heat. When hot, put in the peppercorns, cloves, bay leaves, and cardamom pods. Stir for a second. Now put in the onions, garlic, and ginger. Stir and fry until the onions develop brown specks. Now add the meat, cumin, coriander, cayenne, and 1 teaspoon of the salt. Stir and fry for a minute. Add 1 tablespoon of the beaten yogurt. Stir and fry for another minute. Add another tablespoon of the yogurt. Stir and fry for a minute. Keep doing this until all the yogurt has been incorporated. The meat should also have a slightly browned look. Add the spinach and the remaining 1 teaspoon salt. Stir to mix. Keep stirring and cooking until the spinach wilts completely. Cover tightly and simmer on low heat for about 1 hour 10 minutes or until the meat is tender.

Remove the lid and add the *garam masala*. Turn the heat to medium. Stir and cook another 5 minutes or until most (but not all) the water in the spinach disappears and you have a thick, green sauce.

Note: The whole spices in this dish are not meant to be eaten.

calves' liver in a gingery sauce

Kaleji

You may make this with calves' liver or, if you like, with lambs' or goats' liver. You could, of course, serve it as part of an Indian meal. However, if you are looking for a quick lunch or dinner idea or for something for an after-the-theater supper, serve this on toast with a green salad on the side. You should cut the crusty edges off the slice of bread before toasting it. If you do not mind the calories, frying the bread in oil to make a large crouton makes the liver taste even better! The sauce can be made ahead of time. It is best to brown the liver and fold it into the sauce just before you eat.

Serves 3 to 4

5 cloves garlic, peeled and coarsely chopped

5 cm (2 inch) piece fresh ginger, peeled and coarsely chopped

1–2 fresh, hot green chilies, coarsely sliced

4 tablespoons plus ¾ cup water

5 tablespoons vegetable oil

½ teaspoon cumin seeds

¼ teaspoon *kalonji*

1 good sized onion, peeled and very finely chopped

6 tablespoons plain yogurt

1 medium tomato, finely chopped

Salt

½ teaspoon *garam masala* (page 21)

⅛ teaspoon cayenne pepper

450 g (1 lb) calves' liver, cut into 1 cm (½ inch) thick slices

Freshly ground black pepper

2 tablespoons finely chopped cilantro (optional)

Put the garlic, ginger, green chilies, and 4 tablespoons water into the container of an electric blender or food processor. Blend until you have a paste.

Put 4 tablespoons of the oil in a large frying pan and place over high heat. When hot, put in the cumin seeds and *kalonji*. Ten seconds later, put in the onion. Stir and fry until the onion turns a reddish brown. Add the paste from the blender. Stir and fry it for 2–3 minutes. Put in 1 tablespoon of the yogurt. Stir and cook until the yogurt is incorporated into the sauce. Put in a second tablespoon of yogurt and incorporate it into the sauce in the same way. Do this with all the yogurt. Now put in the tomato. Stir and cook for a minute. Turn heat down to medium. Stir and cook for another 5 minutes. Add ¾ teaspoon salt and the *garam masala* and cayenne. Stir and cook for another 2 minutes. Add about ¾ cup water and bring to a simmer. Turn off heat. This is the sauce. Leave it in the frying pan.

Shortly before eating, pat the liver pieces dry with paper towels. Sprinkle a little salt and lots of black pepper on both sides of the slices of liver. Put the remaining 1 tablespoon oil into a clean, preferably nonstick, frying pan and place over high heat. When very hot, put in the slices of liver in a single layer. As soon as one side has browned, turn the slices over and brown the second side. Do not let the liver cook through and get hard. Remove the liver to a board and cut it into 1 cm (½ inch) cubes. Place the sauce over medium heat. When hot, put in the liver pieces and the cilantro if you are using it. Simmer for 1 minute, stirring once or twice. Serve.

beef baked with yogurt and black pepper

Dum gosht

Ever since the Moguls came to India, there has been a method of cooking that Indians refer to as "*dum.*" Meat (or rice for that matter) is partially cooked in a heavy pot and then covered over with a flat lid. At this stage the pot and lid are sealed with a "rope" made out of very stiff dough. The pot is placed over a gentle fire – generally the last of the charcoals – and more hot charcoals are spread over the lid. The meat proceeds to cook very slowly until it is tender, often in small amounts of liquid (the equivalent of slow oven baking today). So what I have done here is to update a very traditional Mogul recipe, modernizing it to suit our contemporary kitchens. *Dum* dishes do not have a lot of sauce. Ideally, whatever sauce there is should be thick and cling to the meat.

If you like, you could leave out the cayenne in this recipe. That is probably what the early Moguls did. The later Moguls, seduced by the chili peppers brought over from the New World by the Portuguese, used it generously. I love to eat this meat dish with *chapatis* or *parathas* or *naans*. If you prefer rice, then the more moist *pullaos*, such as Mushroom *Pullao* (page 199), would be the perfect accompaniment. You could also make this dish with stewing lamb from the shoulder.

Serves 4 to 6

6 tablespoons vegetable oil

900 g (2 lb) boneless stewing beef from the neck and shoulder, cut into 4 cm (1½ inch) cubes

3 medium onions, peeled and very finely chopped

6 cloves garlic, peeled and very finely chopped

½ teaspoon powdered ginger

⅛ –½ teaspoon cayenne pepper

1 tablespoon paprika

2 teaspoons salt

½ teaspoon very coarsely ground black pepper

275 ml (1¼ cups) plain yogurt, beaten lightly

Preheat the oven to 180°C/350°F/Gas 4.

Put the oil in a wide, flameproof casserole-type pot and place over medium-high heat. When hot, put in as many meat pieces as the pot will hold easily in a single layer. Brown the meat pieces on all sides and set them aside in a deep plate. Brown all the meat this way.

Put the onions and garlic into the same pot and turn the heat down to medium. Stir and fry the onion-garlic mixture for about 10 minutes or until it has browned. Now put in the browned meat as well as any juices that might have accumulated in the plate. Also put in the ginger, cayenne, paprika, salt, and black pepper. Stir for a minute. Now put in the yogurt and bring to a simmer. Cover tightly, first with aluminium foil and then with a lid, and bake in the oven for 1½ hours. The meat should be tender by now. If it is not tender, pour in 150 ml (½ cup) boiling water, cover tightly, and bake another 20–30 minutes or until the meat is tender. Stir the meat gently before serving.

red lamb or beef stew

Rogan josh

Rogan josh gets its name from its rich, red appearance. The red appearance, in turn, is derived from ground red chilies, which are used quite generously in this recipe. If you want your dish to have the right color and not be very hot, combine paprika with cayenne pepper in any proportion that you like. Just make sure that your paprika is fresh and has a good red color. There are many recipes for *rogan josh*. This is probably the simplest of them all. It may be served with an Indian bread or rice. A green bean or eggplant dish would be a perfect accompaniment.

Serves 4 to 6

Two 2.5 cm (1 inch) cubes fresh ginger, peeled and coarsely chopped

8 cloves garlic, peeled

350–470 ml (1^1/$_2$–2 cups) water

10 tablespoons vegetable oil

900 g (2 lb) boned lamb from the shoulder or leg, or stewing beef (chuck), cut into 2.5 cm (1 inch) cubes

10 cardamom pods

2 bay leaves

6 cloves

10 peppercorns

2.5 cm (1 inch) cinnamon stick

2 medium onions, peeled and finely chopped

1 teaspoon ground coriander

2 teaspoons ground cumin

4 teaspoons bright red paprika mixed with ^{1}/$_4$–1 teaspoon cayenne pepper

1^1/$_4$ teaspoons salt

6 tablespoons plain yogurt

^{1}/$_4$ teaspoon *garam masala* (page 21)

Freshly ground black pepper

Put the ginger, garlic, and 4 tablespoons water into the container of an electric blender. Blend well until you have a smooth paste.

Heat the oil in a wide, heavy pot over medium-high heat. Brown the meat cubes in several batches and set to one side. Put the cardamom pods, bay leaves, cloves, peppercorns, and cinnamon into the same hot oil. Stir once and wait until the cloves swell and the bay leaves begin to take on color. This just takes a few seconds. Now put in the onions. Stir and fry for about 5 minutes or until the onions turn a medium-brown color. Put in the ginger-garlic paste and stir for 30 seconds. Then add the coriander, cumin, paprika-cayenne, and salt. Stir and fry for another 30 seconds. Add the fried meat cubes and juices. Stir for 30 seconds. Now put in 1 tablespoon of the yogurt. Stir and fry for about 30 seconds or until the yogurt is well blended. Add the remaining yogurt, a tablespoon at a time as before. Stir and fry for 3–4 minutes.

Now add 275 ml (1^1/$_4$ cups) water if you are cooking lamb and 425 ml (2 cups) water if you are cooking beef. Bring the contents of the pot to a boil, scraping in all browned spices on the sides and bottom of the pot. Cover, turn heat to low and simmer for about an hour for lamb and 2 hours for beef, or until the meat is tender. (It could be baked, covered, in a preheated 180°C/350°F oven for the same length of time or until tender.) Every 10 minutes or so, give the meat a good stir. When the meat is tender, take off the lid, turn the heat up to medium, and boil away some of the liquid. You should end up with tender meat in a thick, reddish brown sauce. Spoon off the fat. Sprinkle *garam masala* and black pepper over the meat before you serve and mix them in.

kashmiri red lamb stew

Kashmiri rogan josh

Kashmiri Hindus do not eat any onions or garlic and they often use dry, powdered ginger instead of the fresh kind. This is their version of *rogan josh*. (For more on *rogan josh*, see the preceding recipe.) I have left the bones in the meat this time. *Kashmiri rogan josh* may be served with Frozen Spinach with Potatoes (page 157), plain long-grain rice, and a relish.

Serves 4 to 6

1 tablespoon fennel seeds

720 ml (3¼ cups) plain yogurt

6 tablespoons vegetable oil

2 cm (¾ inch) cinnamon stick

½ teaspoon cloves

Pinch of ground asafetida (optional)

1 kg 350 g (3 lb) stewing lamb (with bone) from the shoulder and neck, cut into 5 cm (2 inch) cubes

2½ teaspoons salt, or to taste

4 teaspoons bright red paprika mixed with ¼–1 teaspoon cayenne pepper

1½ teaspoons powdered ginger

845 ml (3⅔ cups) water

¼ teaspoon *garam masala* (page 21)

Put the fennel seeds into the container of a spice grinder or clean coffee grinder and grind until fine.

Put the yogurt in a bowl and beat it with a fork or a whisk until it is smooth and creamy.

Put the oil in a large pot and set over high heat. When hot, put in the cinnamon and cloves. A second later, put in the asafetida, if using. A second after that, put in all the meat and the salt. Stir the meat and cook, still over high heat, for about 5 minutes. Now put in the paprika and cayenne and give the meat a good stir. Slowly add the yogurt, a small amount at a time, stirring the meat vigorously as you do so. Add all the yogurt this way. Keep cooking on high heat until all the liquid has boiled away and the meat pieces have browned slightly. Add the fennel and ginger. Give the meat some more good stirs. Now put in the water, cover so as to leave the lid very slightly ajar, and cook on medium heat for 30 minutes. Cover completely and cook on low heat for another 45 minutes or until the meat is tender. Stir a few times, making sure that there is always some liquid in the pan.

Remove the lid and add the *garam masala*. You should have a thick reddish brown sauce. If it is too thin boil some of the liquid away.

delhi-style lamb cooked with potatoes

Aloo gosht

This is one of the everyday meat dishes that I grew up with in Delhi. I still love its honey taste and have a particular weakness for its sauce, which seems to combine all the goodness of lamb, potatoes, tomatoes, and the cheaper, more common Indian spices – cumin, coriander, turmeric, and cayenne pepper. I like it with rice or an Indian bread and Gujerati-style Green Beans (page 131).

Serves 6

7 tablespoons vegetable oil

2 medium onions, peeled and finely chopped

$1/2$–1 fresh, hot green chili, finely chopped

5 cloves garlic, peeled and finely chopped

1 kg ($2^{1}/_{4}$ lb) boned lamb from the shoulder, cut into 2.5 cm (1 inch) cubes

3 medium fresh tomatoes, peeled (page 30) and finely chopped (canned tomatoes may be substituted)

1 tablespoon ground cumin

2 teaspoons ground coriander

$1/2$ teaspoon ground turmeric

$1/4$–1 teaspoon cayenne pepper

2 teaspoons salt

450 g (1 lb) medium-sized potatoes, peeled and cut in half

845 ml ($3^{2}/_{3}$ cups) water

Put the oil in a large, heavy pot and set over high heat. When hot, put in the onions, green chili, and garlic. Stir and fry until the onions have browned slightly.

Put in the meat and stir it vigorously for about 5 minutes. Now put in the tomatoes, cumin, coriander, turmeric, cayenne, and salt. Continue to stir and cook on high heat for 10–15 minutes or until the sauce is thick and the oil seems to separate from it. Add the potatoes and the water. Cover, leaving the lid just very slightly ajar, and cook on medium-low heat for about 1 hour 10 minutes or until the meat is tender and the sauce is thick.

mughlai lamb with turnips

Shabdeg

Turnips are perhaps the most underrated vegetable in the world. This classical Mogul recipe calls for small, whole turnips. The turnips end up by absorbing all the delicious meat juices, turning buttery soft and yet retaining their own rather pretty shape. I like to serve this dish with Mushroom *Pullao* (page 199) and Spicy Green Beans (page 132). *Dal* and a yogurt relish can also be added to the meal.

Serves 6

10 small turnips, weighing 750 g (1½ lb) without leaves and stems (if your turnips are larger, halve them)

2¾ teaspoons salt

5 medium onions, peeled

8 tablespoons vegetable oil

1 kg (2¼ lb) stewing lamb (with bone) from the shoulder, cut into 4 cm (1½ inch) cubes

285 ml (1¼ cups) plain yogurt

2.5 cm (1 inch) piece fresh ginger, peeled and very finely chopped

½ teaspoon ground turmeric

½ teaspoon cayenne pepper

1 tablespoon ground coriander

2.25 liters (10 cups) water

½ teaspoon *garam masala* (page 21)

Peel the turnips and prick them all over with a fork. Put them in a bowl and rub them with ¾ teaspoon of the salt. Set aside for 1½–2 hours.

Cut the onions in half, lengthwise, and then crosswise into very thin slices.

Put the oil in a large, wide, and preferably nonstick pot over medium-high heat. When hot, put in the onions. Stir and fry for about 12 minutes or until the onions are a reddish brown color. Remove the onions with a slotted spoon, squeezing out and leaving behind as much oil as you can. Spread the onions out on a plate. Put the meat into the same pot. Also put in the yogurt, ginger, and 1 teaspoon of the salt. Stir and bring to a boil. Turn the heat up high. You should, at this stage, have a fair amount of rather thin sauce. Cook on high heat, stirring every now and then, for about 10 minutes or until the sauce is fairly thick and you just begin to see the oil. Turn the heat down a bit to medium-high and continue to stir and fry for 5–7 minutes or until the meat is lightly browned and the sauce has disappeared. Turn the heat to medium-low. Put in the turmeric, cayenne, and coriander. Stir for a minute.

Now put in the water and 1 teaspoon of the salt. Drain the turnips and add them as well. Bring the pan to a boil. Turn the heat to medium-high and continue to cook, uncovered, for about 45 minutes or until you have less than a third of the liquid left.

Stir the pot several times during this cooking period.

Put in the browned onions and the *garam masala*. Stir gently to mix and turn heat to low. Cook gently, uncovered, for another 10 minutes. Stir a few times during this period, taking care not to break the turnips.

Spoon off the oil that floats to the top and serve hot.

whole leg of lamb in a spicy yogurt sauce

Raan masaledar

If you are having guests for dinner, this might be the perfect dish to serve. It is quite impressive – a whole leg dressed with a rich sauce, served garnished with almonds and raisins. I often serve it with Sweet Yellow Rice (page 201) and a green vegetable.

You need to buy a 2.25 kg (5 lb) leg of lamb. Get the butcher to remove the H bone and to make a deep pocket to hold a stuffing. (You will not actually stuff the leg but most butchers seem to understand "stuffing" better than they do "spice paste.") Also, ask the butcher to cut the protruding leg bone as close to the end of the meat as possible. This is to enable you to fit it into your baking dish easily. Ask the butcher to remove all the fat on the outside of the leg as well as the parchmentlike skin. (You could, of course, do this yourself.)

For baking, you need a dish large enough to hold the leg easily and about 5–6 cm (2–2½ inches) deep to hold the sauce. Ideally, the dish should have a cover but you can use aluminum foil instead. Ovenproof and stainless steel baking dishes are best as they do not affect the taste of the sauce.

Serves 5 to 6

One 2.25 kg (5 lb) leg of lamb, trimmed (see opposite)

FOR THE SAUCE

5 tablespoons blanched almonds

3 medium onions, peeled and coarsely chopped

8 cloves garlic, peeled

Four 2.5 cm (1 inch) cubes fresh ginger, peeled and coarsely chopped

4 fresh, hot green chilies, coarsely chopped

600 ml (2½ cups) plain yogurt

2 tablespoons ground cumin

4 teaspoons ground coriander

½ teaspoon cayenne pepper

3½ teaspoons salt

½ teaspoon *garam masala* (page 21)

6 tablespoons vegetable oil

½ teaspoon cloves

16 cardamom pods

5 cm (2 inch) cinnamon stick

10 black peppercorns

FOR THE GARNISH

4 tablespoons raisins

2 tablespoons blanched, split or slivered almonds

Make sure that all the fat has been trimmed from the outside of the leg and that most of the fell (parchmentlike white skin) has been pulled off. Put the leg in a baking dish (see opposite).

Put the blanched almonds, onions, garlic, ginger, green chilies, and 3 tablespoons of the yogurt into the container of a food processor or blender and blend to a paste.

Put the remaining yogurt into a bowl. Beat lightly with a fork or a whisk until it is smooth and creamy. Add the paste from the processor, the cumin, coriander, cayenne, salt, and *garam masala*. Mix.

Push some of the spice paste into all the openings in the lamb. Be quite generous about this. Spread the paste evenly on the underside of the leg (the side that originally had less fat). Now, using a small, sharp, pointed knife (such as a paring knife), make deep slashes in the meat and push in the spice paste with your fingers. Turn the leg over so its outer side (the side that was once covered with fat) is on top. Spread a very thick layer of paste over it. Again, make deep slashes with the knife and push the spice paste into the slashes. Pour all the remaining spice paste over and around the meat. Cover with plastic wrap and refrigerate for 24 hours.

Take the baking dish with the meat out of the refrigerator and let the meat come to room temperature. Remove the plastic wrap. Put the oil in a small frying pan and set over medium heat. When hot, put in the cloves, cardamom pods, cinnamon, and peppercorns. When the cloves swell – this takes just a few seconds – pour the hot oil and spices over the leg of lamb.

Preheat the oven to 200°C/400°F.

Cover the baking dish tightly either with its own lid or with a large piece of aluminum foil. Bake, covered, for 1½ hours. Remove the foil and bake uncovered for 45 minutes. Baste 3–4 times with the sauce during this period. Scatter, or arrange in a pattern, the raisins and the 2 tablespoons of almonds over the top of the leg and bake for another 5–6 minutes. Remove the baking dish from the oven and let it sit in a warm place for 15 minutes. Take the leg out of the pan and set it on a warm platter. Spoon off all the fat from the top of the sauce. Use a slotted spoon and fish out all the whole spices in the sauce. Discard the spices. Pour the sauce around the leg.

shahjahani leg of lamb

Shahjahani raan

An exquisite recipe from my friend Usha Ismail that belongs to the very best tradition of Muslim banquet cooking. A whole leg of lamb is marinated for 48 hours in a mixture of yogurt, ginger, and *garam masala*, then cooked very slowly with dried figs, as well as roasted and ground almonds. A paste of roasted poppy seeds and browned onions is added toward the end. You may add peeled potatoes (that have been browned first in a little oil) to the sauce an hour before the cooking ends if you so desire.

I have served this dish at many of my own parties, including one for the first birthday of my grandson (to be eaten by the grown-ups of course: the children had a choice of rice and *dal* or pasta with tomato sauce – as well as the usual cake and ice cream).

If you want the food to have a really festive – and very Indian – aroma, as I often do, sprinkle a little *kewda* essence or *kewda* water over the meat just before you serve it. This is sold only by Indian grocers and comes from a variety of screw pine. Mix about 1 teaspoon of the essence or 1 tablespoon of the water in a few tablespoons of the sauce and spread it over and around the leg. Serve with an elegant rice dish.

Serves 6

One 2.25–2.75 kg (5–6 lb) leg of lamb
900 g (2 lb) plain yogurt
½ medium-sized onion peeled and coarsely chopped, plus 2 medium onions peeled and cut, crosswise, into very fine rings
5 tablespoons peeled, coarsely chopped garlic
About 18 cm (7 inch) piece fresh ginger, peeled and coarsely chopped
5 teaspoons salt
1 teaspoon cayenne pepper
1 tablespoon *garam masala* (page 21)
Blanched, slivered almonds measured to the 300 ml (1¼ cups) mark in a measuring cup
12 dried figs
Vegetable oil for sautéing
6 tablespoons white poppy seeds

Remove all the fell (parchmentlike outer skin) and fat from the leg of lamb. Jab it all over with the point of a sharp knife.

Put all the yogurt into a big bowl (large enough to hold the lamb) and beat lightly with a fork until smooth and creamy. Remove 4 tablespoons of the yogurt and put into the container of an electric blender or food processor. Also put into the blender the chopped ½ onion, the garlic, ginger, salt, cayenne, and *garam masala*. Blend until you have a smooth paste, pushing down with a rubber spatula when necessary. Pour the contents of the blender into the bowl of yogurt and mix well. Put the leg of lamb into the yogurt and rub the marinade into the meat. Cover well and refrigerate for 24–48 hours. (The longer time is ideal though the shorter will do.)

Preheat the oven to 180°C/350°F.

Use a large, round, or oval casserole-type pot or heavy roasting pan. Put the leg of lamb in its center and pour the marinade over and around it. Bring to a simmer on top of the stove. Cover tightly with a lid or a large piece of aluminum foil and put in the oven. Bake, covered, for 1½ hours.

While the lamb bakes, put a cast-iron frying pan over medium heat. When hot, put in the almonds. Stir them until they have roasted lightly. Now grind them in a clean coffee grinder or other spice grinder. Add the almonds to the lamb sauce

after 1½ hours and mix well. Scatter the figs around the leg. Cover again, put the lamb back in the oven, and bake for another 1–1½ hours or until it is quite tender. While the lamb bakes this time, do two things: fry the onions and roast and grind the poppy seeds.

To fry the onions: Line a large plate with paper towels. Put about 5 mm (¼ inch) oil in a medium-sized frying pan and set over medium-high heat. When hot, put in the sliced onions. Stir and fry until the onions start to brown at the edges. Turn heat to medium. Continue to stir and fry until the onions turn reddish brown and crisp. Remove them with a slotted spoon and spread out on the paper towels. (The oil may be reused.)

To roast and grind the poppy seeds: Put a cast-iron frying pan over medium heat. When hot, put in the poppy seeds. Stir and roast until they are a few shades darker. Remove the seeds and allow them to cool slightly. Grind as finely as possible in a clean coffee grinder or other spice grinder.

When the lamb is tender, crumble the onions and add them as well as the ground poppy seeds to the lamb sauce. Mix gently. Spoon some of this sauce over the lamb, cover again, and put back in the oven for another 10 minutes.

To serve: Put the leg of lamb on a large plate used for roasts. Put the figs on another plate for the moment. Spoon off as much fat as you can from the sauce and then ladle this sauce over the leg. Arrange the figs around the meat. Carve the meat at the table.

royal" lamb or beef with a creamy almond sauce

Shahi korma

There are many Indian dishes that were inspired, a few centuries ago, by dishes from other countries. *Shahi korma* – lamb cubes smothered in a rich almond and cream sauce – owes its ancestry to Persian food. It could be served with rice (perhaps Spiced Basmati Rice, page 194) or a bread (*naan*, *chapati* or *paratha*) and a vegetable such as Cauliflower with Potatoes (page 144). For a quick, but elegant, meal you could serve *shahi korma* with plain rice and a crisp green salad. This recipe uses the traditional cooking method, on the top of the stove, but you could do the final long cooking in the oven (particularly useful if you are making a large meal and need the top of the stove for other dishes). Preheat the oven to 180°C/350°F and, once you have combined the meat, salt, cream, and water, and brought it to a boil, you can cover the pan and put it in the oven instead. The cooking times and other general directions remain the same.

Serves 4 to 6

8 cloves garlic, peeled

2.5 cm (1 inch) cube fresh ginger, peeled and coarsely chopped

5 tablespoons blanched, slivered almonds

About 200–225 ml ($^3/_4$–1 cup) water

7 tablespoons vegetable oil

900 g (2 lb) boned lamb from the shoulder or leg or stewing beef (chuck), cut into 2.5 cm (1 inch) cubes

10 whole cardamom pods

6 whole cloves

2.5 cm (1 inch) cinnamon stick

2 medium onions, peeled and finely chopped

1 teaspoon ground coriander seeds

2 teaspoons ground cumin seeds

$^1/_2$ teaspoon cayenne pepper

1$^1/_4$ teaspoons salt

300 ml (10 fl oz) light cream

$^1/_4$ teaspoon *garam masala* (page 21)

Put the garlic, ginger, almonds, and 6 tablespoons water into the container of an electric blender. Blend until you have a paste.

Put the oil in a wide, heavy, preferably nonstick pot and set over medium-high heat. When hot, put in just enough meat pieces so they lie, uncrowded, in a single layer. Brown the meat pieces on all sides, then remove them with a slotted spoon and put them in a bowl. Brown all the meat this way.

Put the cardamom pods, cloves, and cinnamon into the hot oil. Within seconds the cloves will expand. Now put in the onions. Stir and fry the onions until they turn a brownish color. Turn the heat down to medium. Put in the paste from the blender as well as the coriander, cumin, and cayenne. Stir and fry this mixture for 3–4 minutes or until it too has browned somewhat. Now put in the meat cubes as well as any liquid that might have accumulated in the meat bowl, the salt, the cream, and 100 ml ($^1/_2$ cup) water. If you are cooking beef, add another 100 ml ($^1/_2$ cup) water. Bring to a boil. Cover, turn heat to low, and simmer lamb for 1 hour and beef for 2 hours or until the meat is tender. Stir frequently during this cooking period. Skim off any fat that floats to the top. Sprinkle in the *garam masala* and mix.

Note: The whole spices in this dish are not meant to be eaten.

pork sausages cooked in an indian style

Indians cannot, of course, buy sausages in their local bazaars but here is a simple Indian-style recipe that I use when I am rushed to get dinner on the table. Potatoes with Black Pepper (page 153) may be served on the side.

Serves 4

2.5 cm (1 inch) cube fresh ginger, peeled and coarsely chopped

3 cloves garlic, peeled

4 tablespoons water

225 g (¹/₂ lb) small zucchinis

2 tablespoons vegetable oil

225 g (¹/₂ lb) pork sausages

2 small onions, peeled and chopped

1 teaspoon ground cumin

¹/₄ teaspoon cayenne pepper

2 medium tomatoes, peeled (page 30) and finely chopped (a 225 g/8 oz can of tomatoes may be substituted)

¹/₂ teaspoon salt

Put the ginger, garlic, and water into the container of a food processor or blender. Blend until you have a paste.

Quarter the zucchinis, lengthwise, and then cut the strips into 4 cm (1½ inch) lengths.

Put the oil in a large frying pan and set over medium heat. When hot, put in the sausages. Fry, turning the sausages whenever necessary, until brown on all sides. Remove and keep on a plate.

Put the onions into the same oil. Stir and fry until they begin to turn brown at the edges. Add the ginger-garlic paste. Stir and fry for a minute. Put in the cumin and cayenne. Stir a few times and put in the tomatoes. Stir for a minute. Put in the zucchinis and salt. Bring to a simmer, cover, turn heat to low, and cook for 10 minutes.

Cut the sausages into 3 pieces each. Add them to the pan. Cover and cook for about 5 minutes or until the sausages have heated through.

goan-style hot and sour pork
Vindaloo

The Hindus and Muslims of India do not, generally, eat pork – but Indian Christians do. This dish, with its semi-Portuguese name suggesting that the meat is cooked with wine (or vinegar) and garlic, is a contribution from the Konkani-speaking Christians of western India.

Vindaloos, which may be made out of lamb and beef as well, are usually very, very hot. You can control this heat by putting in just as many red chilies as you think you can manage. Serve mounds of fluffy rice on the side.

Serves 6

2 teaspoons cumin seeds

2–3 dried, hot red chilies

1 teaspoon black peppercorns

1 teaspoon cardamom seeds (you may take the seeds out of the pods if you cannot buy them loose)

7.5 cm (3 inch) cinnamon stick

1½ teaspoons black mustard seeds

1 teaspoon fenugreek seeds

5 tablespoons white wine vinegar

1½–2 teaspoons salt

1 teaspoon light brown sugar

10 tablespoons vegetable oil

2 medium onions, peeled and sliced into fine rings

4–6 tablespoons plus 250 ml (1⅓ cups) water

900 g (2 lb) boneless pork from the shoulder, cut into 2.5 cm (1 inch) cubes

2.5 cm (1 inch) cube fresh ginger, peeled and coarsely chopped

1 small, whole head of garlic, with all the cloves separated and peeled (or the equivalent, if using a large head)

1 tablespoon ground coriander

½ teaspoon ground turmeric

Grind the cumin seeds, red chilies, peppercorns, cardamom seeds, cinnamon, black mustard seeds, and fenugreek seeds in a coffee grinder or other spice grinder. Put the ground spices in a bowl. Add the vinegar, salt, and sugar. Mix and set aside.

Put the oil in a wide, heavy pot and set over medium heat. Put in the onions. Fry, stirring frequently, until the onions turn brown and crisp. Remove the onions with a slotted spoon and put them into the container of an electric blender or food processor. (Turn the heat off.) Add 2–3 tablespoons water to the blender and purée the onions. Add this purée to the ground spices in the bowl. (This is the *vindaloo* paste.) It may be made ahead of time and frozen.

Dry off the meat cubes with paper towels and remove large pieces of fat, if any.

Put the ginger and garlic into the container of an electric blender or food processor. Add 2–3 tablespoons water and blend until you have a smooth paste.

Heat the oil remaining in the pot once again over medium-high heat. When hot, put in the pork cubes, a few at a time, and brown them lightly on all sides. Remove each batch with a slotted spoon and keep in a bowl. Do all the pork this way. Now put the ginger-garlic paste into the same pot. Turn down the heat to medium. Stir the paste for a few seconds. Add the coriander and turmeric. Stir for another few seconds. Add the meat, any juices that may have accumulated, as well as the *vindaloo* paste and 250 ml (1 cup) water. Bring to a boil. Cover and simmer gently for an hour or until pork is tender. Stir a few times during this cooking period.

pork chops with chick-peas

Chhole wala gosht

Normally, this hearty, stew-type dish is cooked with cubes of pork cut off from the shoulder. I have substituted the more easily available thin-cut pork chops and added some mushrooms for good measure.

In India, we often ate this dish with what was pronounced as "selice" and was, in reality, *slices* of white bread. (As a child, I had assumed that "selice" was just another Indian word!) I now prefer slices from the crustier French loaf. Beside the bread, you need to serve nothing more than a simple vegetable, cooked in an Indian or English style. A simple salad would also do. This is a perfect dish for a winter's day and is best served in individual bowls or soup plates.

Dried chick-peas can be cooked in many ways. You can soak them overnight before cooking them or you can follow the method that I have used here, which allows the entire dish to be made in the course of a single day.

You may make these pork chops a day ahead of time and just reheat them.

Serves 6

225 g (¹⁄₂ lb) dried chick-peas,
picked over, rinsed, and drained

8 cups plus 3 tablespoons water

4 cm (1¹⁄₂ inch) cube fresh ginger,
peeled and coarsely chopped

5 cloves garlic, peeled

4 tablespoons vegetable oil

900 g (2 lb) thin-cut pork chops

8 cardamom pods

2.5 cm (1 inch) cinnamon stick

2 bay leaves

1 teaspoon cumin seeds

2 medium onions, peeled and coarsely
chopped

1 tablespoon ground cumin

1 tablespoon ground coriander

1 teaspoon ground turmeric

3 medium tomatoes, peeled (page 30)
and chopped

3 medium potatoes, peeled
and cut into 2 cm (³⁄₄ inch) dice

1 tablespoon salt

275 g (10 oz) medium-sized mushrooms,
halved

¹⁄₂ teaspoon cayenne pepper (use more
or less as desired)

Put the chick-peas in a pot. Add 1.75 liters (8 cups) water and bring to a boil. Cover, turn heat to low, and simmer for 2 minutes. Turn off the heat and let the pot sit, covered, for 1 hour. Bring the chick-peas to a boil again. Cover, turn heat to low, and simmer for 1¹⁄₂ hours.

Put the ginger, garlic, and 3 tablespoons water into the container of a food processor or blender. Blend until you have a paste.

Put the oil in a large, wide frying pan and set over medium-high heat. When hot, put in as many pork chops as the pan will hold in a single layer. Brown them on both sides without attempting to cook them through. Remove the chops and put them on a plate.

Put the cardamom pods, cinnamon, bay leaves, and cumin seeds into the hot oil. Immediately, turn the heat down to medium-low. Stir once and put in the onions. Stir and fry the onions for a minute, scraping the hardened pan juices as you do so. Now put in the ginger-garlic paste and stir once. Put in the ground cumin, ground coriander, and turmeric. Stir for a minute. Put in the tomatoes, potatoes, pork chops, and any liquid that may have accumulated in the plate, salt, and the chick-peas and all their cooking liquid. Stir and bring to a boil. Cover, turn heat to low, and simmer for 45 minutes. Add the mushrooms and cayenne. Cover and simmer for 15 minutes.

Note: The large whole spices in this dish should not be eaten.

Since chicken is now mass-produced and fairly cheap, its status has been greatly reduced. This saddens me. I was brought up thinking of chicken as something special and have never managed to get over thinking so; besides, I like chicken. And there are such wonderful ways to cook it, from the simple Spicy Baked Chicken to the elegant *Makkhani murghi* (Chicken in a Butter Sauce) and the very impressive *Murgh musallam* (Whole Chicken Baked in Aluminum Foil). If you are on a diet, you can eat Tandoori-style Chicken, which is cooked without fat, and when you want to indulge yourself, you can dine on *Shahjahani murghi* (Mughlai Chicken with Almonds and Raisins).

There are two things to remember when cooking Indian-style chicken dishes. The first is that we nearly always skin the chicken before we cook it. Skin has never been popular in India, perhaps because it gets so soft and flabby in stews. The second is that, for most of our dishes, we cut up the chicken into fairly small pieces. Legs, for example, are always separated into drumsticks and thighs. Breasts are cut into 4–6 parts. Wings and backs are similarly cut up.

When one of my recipes calls for chicken pieces, you can either buy a whole 1.5 kg (3–3½ lb) chicken and cut it up yourself using a sharp knife and a cleaver or else you can buy chicken parts – the ones you prefer – and cut them up further, if necessary. I happen to have a family in which four members like dark meat and one only likes breast meat (unless it is a roast, when we all prefer breast meat). This does not make life easy. But I do have to keep everyone happy so I frequently resort to buying parts.

poultry and eggs

bombay-style chicken with red split lentils

Murghi aur masoor dal

This dish is really like a hearty stew, just perfect for cold winter days. You could add vegetables such as shelled peas or 1 cm (½ inch) lengths of green beans. Put them in when you add the lemon juice. Traditionally, rice is served on the side but you could serve thickly cut slices of some dark, crusty bread.

Serves 6 to 7

250 g (9 oz) red split lentils (*masoor dal*), picked over, washed, and drained

1 medium onion, peeled and chopped

½–1 fresh, hot green chili, finely sliced

2 teaspoons ground cumin

½ teaspoon ground turmeric

1 teaspoon peeled, very finely chopped ginger

1.5 liters (6⅓ cups) water

About 1 kg 350 g (3 lb) chicken pieces, skinned

2¼ teaspoons salt

2 tablespoons vegetable oil

1 teaspoon cumin seeds

2–4 cloves garlic, peeled and finely chopped

¼–¾ teaspoon cayenne pepper

2 tablespoons lemon juice

½ teaspoon sugar

¼ teaspoon *garam masala* (page 21)

Optional garnish: 3 tablespoons chopped cilantro

Combine the lentils, onion, green chili, ground cumin, turmeric, half of the chopped ginger, and the water in a big, heavy pot. Bring to a simmer, cover, leaving the lid very slightly ajar, and cook on low heat for 45 minutes. Add the chicken pieces and the salt. Mix and bring to a boil. Cover, turn heat to low, and simmer gently for 25–30 minutes or until the chicken is tender.

Put the oil in a small frying pan and set over medium heat. When hot, put in the cumin seeds. As soon as the seeds begin to sizzle – this just takes a few seconds – put in the remaining ½ teaspoon chopped ginger and the garlic. Fry until the garlic turns slightly brown. Now put in the cayenne. Lift up the frying pan immediately and pour its entire contents – oil and spices – into the pot with the chicken and lentils. Also add the lemon juice, sugar, and *garam masala*. Stir to mix and cook on medium-low heat for 5 minutes.

Sprinkle the cilantro over the top, if you wish, just before you serve.

tandoori-style chicken

Tandoori murghi

I have, I think, found a way to make tandoori-style chicken without a *tandoor*! The *tandoor*, as I am sure you all know by now, is a vat-shaped clay oven, heated with charcoal or wood. The heat inside builds up to such an extent that small whole chickens, skewered and thrust into it, cook in about 10 minutes. This fierce heat seals the juices of the bird and keeps it moist while an earlier marinating process ensures that the chicken is tender and well flavored. The result is quite spectacular.

To approximate a *tandoor*, I use an ordinary oven, preheated to its maximum temperature. Then, instead of cooking a whole bird, I use serving-sized pieces – legs that are cut into two and breasts that are quartered. The cooking time is not 10 minutes because home ovens do not get as hot as *tandoors*. Still, breasts cook in about 15–20 minutes and legs in 20–25 minutes.

Tandoori chicken may, of course, be served just the way it comes out of the oven with a few wedges of lemon, or it can, without much effort, be transformed into *Makkhani murghi* (see next recipe) by smothering it with a rich butter-cream-tomato sauce. Both dishes are excellent for dinner parties as most of the work can be done a day ahead of time. The chicken is marinated the night before so all you have to do on the day of the party is to cook it in the oven for a brief 20–25 minutes just before you sit down to eat. If you wish to make the sauce, all the ingredients for it except the butter may be combined in a bowl the day before and refrigerated. After that, the sauce cooks in less than 5 minutes and involves only one step – heating it.

Both these chicken dishes may be served with rice or *naan* and a green bean or cauliflower dish.

Note: The traditional orange color of cooked tandoori chicken comes from food coloring. You may or may not want to use it. If you do, mix yellow and red liquid food colors to get a bright orange shade. If your red is very dark, use only ½ tablespoon of it.

Serves 4 to 6

1 kg 125 g (2½ lb) chicken pieces, skinned (you may use legs, breasts, or a combination of the two)

1 teaspoon salt

1 juicy lemon

425 ml (1¾ cups) plain yogurt

½ medium-sized onion, peeled and quartered

1 clove garlic, peeled

2 cm (¾ inch) cube fresh ginger, peeled and quartered

½ fresh, hot green chili, roughly sliced

2 teaspoons *garam masala* (page 21)

3 tablespoons yellow liquid food coloring mixed with ½–1½ tablespoons red liquid food coloring (optional, see opposite)

Lime wedges (optional)

Cut each leg into 2 pieces and each breast into 4 pieces. Cut 2 long slits on each side of each part of the legs. The slits should never start at an edge and they should be deep enough to reach the bone. Cut similar slits on the meaty side of each breast piece.

Spread the chicken pieces out on one or two large platters. Sprinkle half the salt and squeeze the juice from three-quarters of the lemon over them. Lightly rub the salt and lemon juice into the slits. Turn the chicken pieces over and do the same on the other side with the remaining salt and lemon juice. Set aside for 20 minutes.

Combine the yogurt, onion, garlic, ginger, green chili, and *garam masala* in the container of an electric blender or food processor. Blend until you have a smooth paste. Empty the paste into a strainer placed over a large ceramic or stainless steel bowl. Push the paste through.

Brush the chicken pieces on both sides with the food coloring and then put them with any accumulated juices and any remaining food coloring into the bowl with the marinade. Mix well, making sure that the marinade goes into the slits in the chicken. Cover and refrigerate for 6–24 hours (the longer the better). Preheat the oven to its maximum temperature.

Take the chicken pieces out of the bowl, shaking off as much of the marinade as possible. Arrange them in a large shallow baking pan in a single layer. Bake for 20–25 minutes or until just done. You might test the chicken with a fork just to be sure. Serve hot, with lime wedges if you wish.

Note: The leftover marinade may be frozen and reused *once*.

chicken in a butter sauce

Makkhani murghi

The sauce in this dish should be folded into the butter at the very last minute as it tends to separate otherwise. However, you can combine all the ingredients except the butter up to a day ahead of time and refrigerate them until they are needed.

This is a wonderfully simple but spectacular dish in which the Tandoori-style Chicken of the preceding recipe is transformed with a sauce.

Serves 4 to 6

4 tablespoons tomato purée

Water to mix

2.5 cm (1 inch) cube fresh ginger, peeled and grated very finely to a pulp

300 ml (10 fl oz) light cream

1 teaspoon *garam masala* (page 21)

³/₄ teaspoon salt

¹/₄ teaspoon sugar

1 fresh, hot green chili, finely chopped

¹/₄ teaspoon cayenne pepper

1 tablespoon very finely chopped cilantro

4 teaspoons lemon juice

1 teaspoon ground, roasted cumin seeds (page 20)

100 g (¹/₂ cup) unsalted butter

Tandoori-style Chicken, freshly cooked according to the preceding recipe

Put the tomato purée in a clear measuring cup. Add water slowly, mixing as you go, to make up 250 ml (1 cup) of tomato sauce. Add the ginger, cream, *garam masala*, salt, sugar, green chili, cayenne, cilantro, lemon juice, and ground, roasted cumin seeds. Mix well.

Heat the butter in a wide sauté pan or a large frying pan. When the butter has melted, add all the ingredients in the measuring cup. Bring to a simmer and cook on medium heat for a minute, mixing in the butter as you do so. Add the chicken pieces (but not their accumulated juices). Stir once and put the chicken pieces on a warm serving platter. Extra sauce should be spooned over the top.

chicken in a fried onion sauce

Murghi rasedar

This is how I cook the dish that my children used to refer to as our "everyday" chicken. We tend to eat it with Plain Basmati Rice (page 193) and Carrot and Onion Salad (page 217).

Serves 4 to 6

1 kg 125 g (2½ lb) chicken parts

4 medium onions, peeled

4 cm (1½ inch) cube fresh ginger, peeled and coarsely chopped

6 cloves garlic, peeled

7 tablespoons vegetable oil

1 tablespoon ground coriander

1 tablespoon ground cumin

½ teaspoon ground turmeric

¼–½ teaspoon cayenne pepper

4 tablespoons plain yogurt

570 ml (2½ cups) water

2 medium tomatoes, peeled (page 30) and very finely chopped (canned tomatoes may be substituted)

2 teaspoons salt

½ teaspoon *garam masala* (page 21)

1 tablespoon finely chopped cilantro (parsley may be substituted)

Cut the chicken into serving pieces. Whole legs should be separated into drumsticks and thighs. Whole breasts should be cut into 4–6 pieces. Skin all the chicken pieces.

Chop half of the onions coarsely. Cut the remaining onions into halves, lengthwise, and then crosswise into very thin slices.

Put the chopped onions, ginger, and garlic into the container of an electric blender. Blend to a paste.

Put the oil in a large, wide sauté pan or a large, deep frying pan (preferably nonstick) and set over medium heat. When hot, put in the sliced onions. Stir and fry the onions until they are a deep, reddish brown color. Remove the onions with a slotted spoon, squeezing out and leaving behind as much of the oil as possible. Put on a plate and set aside.

Take the pan off the heat. Put in the paste (keep face averted). Put the pan back on the heat. Stir and fry the paste until it is brown, about 3–4 minutes. Now put in the ground coriander, cumin, turmeric, and cayenne and stir once. Put in 1 tablespoon of the yogurt. Stir for about 30 seconds or until it is incorporated in the sauce. Add all the yogurt this way. Add the chicken pieces and stir them around for a minute.

Pour in the water, add the tomatoes and salt. Stir to mix and bring to a simmer. Cover, turn heat to low, and cook for 20 minutes. Sprinkle in the *garam masala* and the fried onions. Mix. Cook, uncovered, on medium heat for 7–8 minutes or until the sauce reduces and thickens.

Skim off the fat and put the chicken in a warm serving dish. Sprinkle the cilantro or parsley over the top.

spicy baked chicken

Masaledar murghi

Here is one of those easy chicken dishes that can be prepared almost effortlessly. There is a marinating period, though, of about 3 hours.

This chicken has a very red look, which it gets from ground, hot red chilies. To get the same effect — and not all of the heat — you can combine paprika with cayenne pepper in any proportion that you like as long as the total quantity is about 1½ tablespoons. I like to serve this chicken with Rice and Peas (page 196) and Red Split Lentils with Cumin Seeds (page 165).

This is one of the few times that I leave the skin on the chicken pieces. It helps to keep them moist in the oven.

Serves 6

1 tablespoon ground cumin

1 tablespoon paprika

1½ teaspoons cayenne pepper (see above)

1 tablespoon ground turmeric

1–1½ teaspoons freshly ground black pepper

2½–3 teaspoons salt, or to taste

2–3 cloves garlic, peeled and mashed to a pulp

6 tablespoons lemon juice

1 kg 500 g (3½ lb) chicken pieces

3 tablespoons vegetable oil

Combine the cumin, paprika, cayenne, turmeric, black pepper, salt, garlic, and lemon juice in a bowl. Mix well. Rub this mixture over the chicken pieces, pushing the paste inside any flaps and openings that you can find. Stuff some paste along the bone of the drumsticks. Spread the chicken pieces in a shallow baking pan, skinside down, and set aside in a cool place for 3 hours.

Preheat the oven to 200°C/400°F.

Brush the tops of the chicken pieces with the oil. Put the chicken in the oven and bake for 20 minutes. Turn the chicken pieces over and bake another 25 minutes or until the chicken is tender. Baste the chicken pieces with the drippings 3–4 times. If a lot of liquid accumulates in your baking pan, remove the extra fat with a spoon. Then pour the remaining liquid into a small saucepan. Boil down until the sauce is somewhat reduced. Arrange the chicken pieces on a platter, pour the reduced sauce over them, and serve at once.

lemony chicken with cilantro

Hare masale wali murghi

Here is a delightful lemony, gingery dish that requires quite a lot of cilantro.
I generally serve it with Spiced Basmati Rice (page 194).

Serves 6

Two 2.5 cm (1 inch) cubes fresh ginger,
peeled and coarsely chopped

240 ml (1 cup) water

6 tablespoons vegetable oil

1 kg 175 g (2½ lb) chicken pieces, skinned

5 cloves garlic, peeled and
very finely chopped

200 g (3 cups) cilantro (weight
without roots and lower stems),
very finely chopped

½–1 fresh, hot green chili,
very finely chopped

¼ teaspoon cayenne pepper

2 teaspoons ground cumin

1 teaspoon ground coriander

½ teaspoon ground turmeric

1 teaspoon salt, or to taste

2 tablespoons lemon juice

Put the ginger and 4 tablespoons water into the container of an electric blender. Blend until you have a paste.

Put the oil in a wide, heavy, preferably nonstick, pot over medium-high heat. When hot, put in as many chicken pieces as the pot will hold in a single layer and brown on both sides. Remove the chicken pieces with a slotted spoon and put them in a bowl. Brown all the chicken pieces this way.

Put the garlic into the same hot oil. As soon as the pieces turn a medium-brown color, turn heat to medium and pour in the paste from the blender. Stir and fry it for a minute. Now add the cilantro, green chili, cayenne, ground cumin, ground coriander, turmeric, and salt. Stir and cook for a minute. Put in all the chicken pieces as well as any liquid that might have accumulated in the chicken bowl. Also add 150 ml (⅔ cup) water and the lemon juice. Stir and bring to a boil. Cover tightly, turn heat to low, and cook for 15 minutes. Turn the chicken pieces over. Cover again and cook another 10–15 minutes or until the chicken is tender.

If the sauce is too thin, uncover the pan and boil some of it away over a slightly higher heat.

mughlai chicken with almonds and raisins

Shahjahani murghi

This elegant, mild dish is very suitable for dinner parties. It could be accompanied by Spiced Basmati Rice (page 194), Cauliflower with Potatoes (page 144), and Yogurt with Walnuts and Cilantro (page 211).

Serves 6

2.5 cm (1 inch) cube fresh ginger, peeled and coarsely chopped

8–9 cloves garlic, peeled

6 tablespoons blanched, slivered almonds

4 tablespoons water

7 tablespoons vegetable oil

1 kg 350 g (3 lb) chicken pieces, skinned

10 cardamom pods

2.5 cm (1 inch) cinnamon stick

2 bay leaves

5 cloves

2 medium onions, peeled and finely chopped

2 teaspoons ground cumin

1/8 –1/2 teaspoon cayenne pepper

7 tablespoons plain yogurt

300 ml (10 oz) light cream

1 1/2 teaspoons salt

1–2 tablespoons golden raisins

1/4 teaspoon *garam masala* (page 21)

Put the ginger, garlic, 4 tablespoons of the almonds, and the water into the container of an electric blender and blend until you have a paste.

Put the oil in a wide, preferably nonstick, pot or deep frying pan and set over medium-high heat. When hot, put in as many chicken pieces as the pan will hold in a single layer. Let the chicken pieces turn golden brown on the bottom. Now turn all the pieces over and brown the second side. Remove the chicken pieces with a slotted spoon and put them in a bowl. Brown all the chicken pieces this way.

Put the cardamom pods, cinnamon, bay leaves, and cloves into the same hot oil. Stir and fry them for a few seconds. Now put in the onions. Stir and fry the onions for 3–4 minutes or until they are lightly browned. Put in the paste from the blender and the cumin and cayenne. Stir and fry for 2–3 minutes or until the oil seems to separate from the spice mixture and the spices are lightly browned. Add 1 tablespoon of the yogurt. Stir and fry it for about 30 seconds. Now add another tablespoon of yogurt. Keep doing this until all the yogurt has been incorporated.

Put in the chicken pieces, any liquid that might have accumulated in the chicken bowl, the cream, and salt. Bring to a simmer. Cover, turn heat to low, and cook gently for 20 minutes. Add the raisins and turn the chicken pieces. Cover and cook another 10 minutes or until the chicken is tender. Add the *garam masala*. Stir to mix.

Put the remaining almonds on a baking pan and put them under the broiler until they brown lightly. You have to toss them frequently. Sprinkle these almonds over the chicken when you serve. Extra fat may be spooned off the top just before serving.

Note: The whole spices in this dish should not be eaten.

chicken with cream

Malai wali murghi

This rich, creamy dish may be served with Eggplant Cooked in the Pickling Style
(page 136) and rice.

Serves 6

1½ teaspoons salt

2 teaspoons ground cumin

1½ teaspoons ground coriander

½ teaspoon ground turmeric

½ teaspoon cayenne pepper

Freshly ground black pepper

1 kg 350 g (3 lb) chicken pieces, skinned

6–7 cloves garlic, peeled

2.5 cm (1 inch) cube fresh ginger, peeled and coarsely chopped

320 ml (1½ cups) water

6 tablespoons vegetable oil

1 medium onion, peeled and finely chopped

2 medium tomatoes, peeled (page 30) and finely chopped

4 tablespoons plain yogurt

1 teaspoon *garam masala* (page 21)

6 tablespoons heavy cream

Sprinkle ½ teaspoon of the salt, 1 teaspoon of the cumin, ½ teaspoon of the coriander, ¼ teaspoon of the turmeric, ¼ teaspoon of the cayenne, and some black pepper on the chicken pieces. Mix well and set aside for at least 1 hour.

Put the garlic and ginger into the container of an electric blender or food processor. Add 120 ml (½ cup) of the water and blend until fairly smooth.

Put the oil in a wide, preferably nonstick, pot and set over medium-high heat. When hot, put in as many chicken pieces as the pot will hold easily in a single layer and brown lightly on both sides. Remove with a slotted spoon and set aside in a bowl. Brown all the chicken pieces the same way.

Put the chopped onion into the remaining oil. Stir and fry until the pieces turn a medium-brown color. Add the garlic-ginger paste. Stir and fry until all the water from the paste evaporates and you see the oil again. Put in the remaining 1 teaspoon cumin, 1 teaspoon coriander, ¼ teaspoon turmeric, and ¼ teaspoon cayenne. Stir and fry for about 20 seconds. Now put in the chopped tomatoes. Turn the heat down to medium-low. Stir and cook the spice paste for 3–4 minutes, mashing the tomato pieces with the back of a slotted spoon as you do so. Add the yogurt, a tablespoon at a time, incorporating it into the sauce each time before you add any more. Put in the chicken pieces and any accumulated juices, the remaining 200 ml (1 cup) water, and 1 teaspoon salt. Bring to a boil. Cover, turn heat to low, and simmer for 20 minutes. Take off the cover. Add the *garam masala* and cream. Mix gently.

Turn the heat up to medium high and cook, stirring gently every now and then, until the sauce has reduced somewhat and has turned fairly thick.

chicken with tomatoes and garam masala

Timatar murghi

This simple chicken dish used to be a great favorite with our children. I generally serve it with Plain Long-grain Rice (page 192) and Whole Green Lentils with Garlic and Onion (page 167).

Serves 6

5 tablespoons vegetable oil

³/₄ teaspoon cumin seeds

2.5 cm (1 inch) cinnamon stick

6 cardamom pods

2 bay leaves

¹/₄ teaspoon peppercorns

2 medium onions, peeled and finely chopped

6–7 cloves garlic, peeled and finely chopped

2.5 cm (1 inch) cube fresh ginger, peeled and finely chopped

6 medium tomatoes, peeled (page 30) and finely chopped (canned tomatoes may be substituted)

1 kg 350 g (3 lb) chicken pieces, skinned

1¹/₂ teaspoons salt

¹/₈ –¹/₂ teaspoon cayenne pepper

¹/₂ teaspoon *garam masala* (page 21)

Put the oil in a large, wide pot and set over medium-high heat. When hot, put in the cumin seeds, cinnamon, cardamom pods, bay leaves, and peppercorns. Stir once and then put in the onions, garlic, and ginger. Stir this mixture until the onions pick up brown specks. Now put in the tomatoes, chicken pieces, salt, and cayenne pepper. Stir to mix and bring to a boil. Cover tightly, turn heat to low, and simmer for 25 minutes or until the chicken is tender. Stir a few times during this cooking period. Remove cover and turn up heat to medium.

Sprinkle in the *garam masala* and cook, stirring gently, for about 5 minutes in order to reduce the liquid in the pot somewhat.

Note: The whole spices in this dish should not be eaten.

goan-style chicken with roasted coconut

Shakoothi

I just love this dish. I ate it for the first time in balmy, palm-fringed, coastal Goa, and have been hoarding the recipe ever since. Even though there are several steps to the recipe, it is not at all hard to put together, especially if you have grated coconut sitting around in the freezer, as I always have. I am now in the habit of buying two or three coconuts whenever I see any good ones. I grate them as soon as I get home (for instructions, see page 18) and then store the grated flesh in flattened plastic bags. Defrosting takes no time at all. This way, I am always ready, not only to make *shakoothi*, but to sprinkle fresh coconut over meats and vegetables whenever I want to.

You could serve this dish with Plain Long-grain Rice (page 192), Spicy Green Beans (page 132) and Onion Relish (page 221).

Serves 4 to 5

1¹⁄₂ tablespoons coriander seeds

1¹⁄₂ teaspoons cumin seeds

1 teaspoon black mustard seeds

2.5 cm (1 inch) cinnamon stick, broken into 3–4 pieces

4 cloves

¹⁄₄ teaspoon black peppercorns

About ¹⁄₆ nutmeg

1 dried, hot red chili
(remove seeds if you want it mild)

240 g (2 cups) grated fresh coconut

6–8 cloves garlic, peeled

2.5 cm (1 inch) cube fresh ginger, peeled and coarsely chopped

¹⁄₂–1 fresh, hot green chili

4 tablespoons plus 300 ml
(1¹⁄₂ cups) water

4 tablespoons vegetable oil

2 medium onions, peeled and minced

1 kg 175 g (2¹⁄₄ lb) chicken pieces, skinned

1¹⁄₂ teaspoons salt

Put the coriander seeds, cumin seeds, mustard seeds, cinnamon, cloves, peppercorns, nutmeg, and red chili in a small, preferably cast-iron frying pan. Place the pan over medium heat. Now quickly "dry-roast" the spices, stirring them frequently until they emit a very pleasant roasted aroma. Empty the spices into a clean coffee grinder or spice grinder and grind until fine. Take the spices out and put them in a bowl.

Put the coconut into the same frying pan and dry-roast it over medium heat, stirring it all the time. The coconut should pick up lots of brown flecks and also smell roasted. Put the coconut in the bowl with the other dry-roasted spices.

Put the garlic, ginger, and green chili into the container of an electric blender, along with 4 tablespoons water. Blend until you have a paste.

Put the oil in a 25–30 cm (10–12 inch) frying pan or sauté pan and set over medium-high heat. When hot, put in the onions. Stir and fry them until they pick up brown spots. Now pour in the garlic-ginger mixture from the blender and stir once. Turn heat to medium. Put in the chicken pieces and salt, as well as the spice-coconut mixture in the bowl. Stir and fry the chicken for 3–4 minutes or until it loses its pinkness and turns slightly brown. Add 300 ml (1¹⁄₄ cups) water and bring to a simmer. Cover tightly, turn heat to low, and cook for 25–30 minutes or until the chicken is tender. Stir a few times during this cooking period, making sure that you turn over each piece of chicken so that it gets evenly colored.

chicken in a red sweet pepper sauce

Lal masale wali murghi

Many of the meat, poultry, and fish dishes that are traditional along India's west coast have thick and stunningly red-looking sauces. The main ingredient, which provides both the texture and the color, is red chilies – fresh or dried. It is almost impossible to find the correct variety of red chili in the West – one that is bright red and just mildly hot. What I have discovered is that a combination of red peppers and cayenne pepper works exceedingly well!

I like to serve this dish with Aromatic Yellow Rice (page 200) and Yogurt with Eggplant (page 212).

Serves 4

1 kg (2¼ lb) chicken pieces

1 large onion, peeled and coarsely chopped

2.5 cm (1 inch) cube fresh ginger, peeled and coarsely chopped

3 cloves garlic, peeled

25 g (2½ tablespoons) blanched, slivered almonds

350 g (¾ lb) red sweet peppers, trimmed, seeded, and coarsely chopped

1 tablespoon ground cumin

2 teaspoons ground coriander

½ teaspoon ground turmeric

⅛ –½ teaspoon cayenne pepper

2 teaspoons salt

7 tablespoons vegetable oil

250 ml (1 cup) water

2 tablespoons lemon juice

½ teaspoon coarsely ground black pepper

If chicken legs are whole, divide drumsticks from thighs with a sharp knife. Breasts should be cut into 4 parts. Skin all chicken pieces.

Combine the onion, ginger, garlic, almonds, peppers, cumin, coriander, turmeric, cayenne, and salt in the container of a food processor or blender. Blend, pushing down with a rubber spatula whenever you need to, until you have a paste.

Put the oil in a large, wide, preferably nonstick, pot and set over medium-high heat. When hot, pour in all the paste. Stir and fry it for 10–12 minutes or until you see the oil forming tiny bubbles around it.

Put in the chicken, with the water, lemon juice, and black pepper. Stir to mix and bring to a boil. Cover, turn heat to low and simmer gently for 25 minutes or until the chicken is tender. Stir a few times.

chicken with roasted coriander in a coconut curry sauce

Dakshini murgh

Here I have combined roasted seeds — coriander, fenugreek, and black pepper —
with coconut milk to make a southern-style chicken. It has a good amount of delicious
sauce, so eat it with rice and a vegetable of your choice. This is an ideal dish for
entertaining. You could easily make it part of a more elaborate menu.

Serves 4

3 tablespoons coriander seeds

$\frac{1}{4}$ teaspoon fenugreek seeds

2 teaspoons black peppercorns

6 tablespoons vegetable oil

1 teaspoon black mustard seeds

5 cm (2 inch) cinnamon stick

1.5 kg (3$\frac{1}{2}$ lb) chicken pieces, skinned
and cut into small serving portions

2 medium-sized onions, peeled
and cut into fine rings

4–5 cloves garlic, peeled and
cut into fine slivers

1 teaspoon peeled, very finely grated
fresh ginger

1 medium tomato, finely chopped

$\frac{1}{2}$ teaspoon ground turmeric

1 teaspoon cayenne pepper

1$\frac{1}{2}$ teaspoons salt

1 tablespoon lemon juice

One 400 g (14 oz) can of coconut milk

2 fresh, hot green chilies,
split in half, lengthwise

Set a small, cast-iron frying pan over medium-high heat for 2–3 minutes.
Now put the coriander seeds, fenugreek seeds, and peppercorns into it. Stir and
roast them for about 1$\frac{1}{2}$ minutes or until they are lightly browned and emit a
roasted aroma. Remove the spices, leave them to cool slightly, then grind them
finely in a clean coffee grinder or other spice grinder.

Put the oil in a wide, preferably nonstick, pot and set over medium-high heat.
When hot, put in the black mustard seeds and cinnamon. As soon as the
mustard seeds begin to pop — this takes just a few seconds — put in the chicken
pieces, only as many as the pot can hold easily in a single layer. Brown the
chicken pieces in as many batches as necessary and remove to a bowl.

Once all the chicken is browned, put the onions and garlic into the same pot
and turn heat to medium. Stir and fry until the onions are light brown. Now put
in the ginger and tomato. Stir and cook until the tomato is soft. Turn heat down.
Add the roasted spice mixture, turmeric, cayenne, salt, and lemon juice. Remove
the very thick coconut cream that will have congealed at the top of the coconut
milk can and set aside. Stir the remaining contents of the can. Add enough
water to fill the can again and pour this mixture over the chicken. Bring to a
boil. Cover, turn heat to low, and simmer for 25 minutes, stirring now and then.

Stir the thick coconut cream that you removed and add that and the green
chilies to the chicken. Stir once or twice as the cream warms through. Turn off
the heat.

Note: The green chilies may be left as a garnish or eaten by those who are
up to it.

whole chicken baked in aluminum foil

Murgh musallam

Over the years, as I am more and more rushed for time, I find myself simplifying some of my own recipes. The traditional *murgh musallam* recipe, for example, is quite a complicated one. I now cook it relatively simply, by smothering a marinated bird with a spice paste, wrapping it in foil, and popping it into the oven. It works beautifully.
I like to serve this dish with Mushroom *Pullao* (page 199), Spinach Cooked with Onions (page 156), and Yogurt with Cucumber and Mint (page 210).

Serves 4 to 6

FOR THE MARINADE

2.5 cm (1 inch) cube fresh ginger, peeled and coarsely chopped

2 large cloves garlic, peeled

6 tablespoons plain yogurt

1/2 teaspoon ground turmeric

1 1/4 teaspoons salt

1/4 – 1/2 teaspoon cayenne pepper

Freshly ground black pepper

YOU ALSO NEED

One 1 kg 50 g (3 1/2 lb) chicken

3 medium onions

4 cloves garlic, peeled

4 cm (1 1/2 inch) cube fresh ginger, peeled and coarsely chopped

2 1/2 tablespoons blanched, slivered almonds

2 teaspoons ground cumin

2 teaspoons ground coriander

1/2 teaspoon ground turmeric

1 tablespoon paprika

1/4 teaspoon cayenne pepper

1 1/2 teaspoons salt

8 tablespoons vegetable oil

2 tablespoons lemon juice

1/2 teaspoon coarsely ground black pepper

1/2 teaspoon *garam masala* (page 21)

Make the marinade: Put the ginger, garlic, and 3 tablespoons of the yogurt into the container of a food processor or electric blender. Blend, pushing down with a rubber spatula whenever you need to, until you have a paste. Add the turmeric, salt, cayenne, and black pepper. Blend for a second to mix. Empty the marinade into a bowl. (Do not wash out the food processor or blender yet.) Add the remaining 3 tablespoons of the yogurt to the marinade and beat it in with a fork.

Skin the entire chicken with the exception of the wing tips. Skin the neck. Put the chicken, breast up, on a platter and put the giblets somewhere near it. Rub the chicken, inside and out, as well as the giblets, with the marinade. Set aside, unrefrigerated, for 2 hours.

Meanwhile, put the onions, garlic, ginger, and almonds into the food processor or blender. Blend, pushing down with a rubber spatula whenever you need to, until you have a paste. Add the cumin, coriander, turmeric, paprika, cayenne, and salt. Blend again to mix.

Put the oil in a large, nonstick frying pan and set over medium-high heat. When hot, put in the paste from the food processor or blender. Fry, stirring, for 8–9 minutes. Add the lemon juice, black pepper, and *garam masala*. Mix. Turn off the heat and let the paste cool.

Preheat the oven to 180°C/350°F.

When the chicken has finished sitting in its marinade for 2 hours, spread out a piece of aluminum foil, large enough to enclose the chicken. Put the chicken, breast up, in the center of the foil and put the giblets somewhere near it. Rub the chicken, inside and out, as well as the giblets, with the fried spice paste. Bring the ends of the foil toward the center to form a tight package. All "seams" should be 5 cm (2 inches) above the "floor" of the package.

Put the wrapped chicken, breast up, on a baking pan and bake in the oven for 1 1/2 hours or until the chicken is tender.

turkey kebabs

Turkey ke kabab

Kebabs can be made out of almost any meat. As turkey is so easily available and is lower in saturated fat than many red meats, I have taken to using it at least once or twice a month.

These kebabs are best put into pockets of pita bread along with Cilantro Chutney (page 218), some sliced onions and tomatoes, and a squeeze of lemon juice, or wrapped in *parathas*. They are an ideal food to take on picnics. If you wish to serve them with drinks make the patties much smaller.

Makes 6 kebabs

450 g (1 lb) finely ground turkey (put twice through the grinder)

12 tablespoons fine, dry breadcrumbs

³/₄ teaspoon salt

³/₄ teaspoon *garam masala* (page 21)

¹/₂ teaspoon cumin seeds

¹/₂ teaspoon coriander seeds

¹/₂ cup finely chopped cilantro

2–3 fresh, hot green chilies, finely chopped

¹/₂ medium onion, peeled and finely chopped

2 teaspoons peeled, finely grated fresh ginger

¹/₂ medium fresh tomato, finely chopped

¹/₄–¹/₂ teaspoon cayenne pepper

Vegetable oil to line the bottom of a frying pan

Lemon wedges

Combine the turkey, 4 tablespoons of the breadcrumbs, salt, *garam masala*, cumin seeds, coriander seeds, cilantro, green chilies, onion, ginger, tomato, and cayenne in a bowl. Mix well and form six 7.5 cm (3 inch) patties. Put the remaining 8 tablespoons breadcrumbs on a plate and dip each patty in them. There should be a thin layer of crumbs on all sides. Cover and refrigerate the patties in a single layer until needed.

Put enough oil in a large frying pan to cover the bottom lightly and set over medium-high heat. When hot, put in the patties – only as many as the pan will hold easily in a single layer. Cook for 3 minutes on each side. Turn heat to medium and cook for another 2–3 minutes on each side.

Eat the patties with generous squeezes of lemon juice.

eggs

The egg recipes in this chapter are simple and tasty, perfect for everyday cooking. If you are looking for a new, spicier approach to eggs, you could try *Ekoori*, scrambled eggs cooked with fresh green coriander and tomato, or the pielike Parsi omelette seasoned with cumin and green chilies. Indians also know how to convert plain, hard-boiled eggs into the most delicious main courses by putting them into thick, creamy sauces or tart, vinegary ones.

spicy scrambled eggs

Ekoori

Ekoori is the Parsi name for them but scrambled eggs, cooked in a similar style, are eaten all over India. Eat them with toast or any Indian bread.

Serves 4

3 tablespoons unsalted butter or vegetable oil

1 small onion, peeled and finely chopped

1/2 teaspoon peeled, very finely grated fresh ginger

1/2 –1 fresh, hot green chili, finely chopped

1 tablespoon very finely chopped cilantro

1/8 teaspoon ground turmeric

1/2 teaspoon ground cumin

1 small tomato, peeled (page 30) and chopped

6 large eggs, lightly beaten

Salt and freshly ground black pepper to taste

Melt the butter in a medium-sized, preferably nonstick, frying pan over medium heat. Put in the onion and sauté until soft. Add the ginger, chili, cilantro, turmeric, cumin, and tomato.

Stir and cook for 3–4 minutes or until the tomatoes are soft.

Put in the beaten eggs. Salt and pepper them lightly. Stir the eggs very gently until they form soft, thick curds.

Cook the scrambled eggs to any consistency you like.

vegetable omelette

Parsi omlate

The Parsis who settled on India's west coast around the Bombay area came originally from Persia over a thousand years ago. Even though they have proudly retained their religion, Zoroastrianism, they have been unafraid to let their adopted country or, for that matter, British colonialists, influence them in their choice of dress, language, and food. The Parsi culinary tradition is unique, borrowing freely as it does from Gujeratis, Maharashtrians, and the English. But there is a Persian streak in there as well. This can best be seen in the fondness for eggs and the abundance of egg dishes – eggs over fried okra, eggs over matchstick potatoes, eggs over tomato chutney – the list is long. Parsis also make all kinds of omelettes. Some are folded in the traditional way but many others are round and pielike. The recipe here is for a pielike omelette, filled with vegetables.

This omelette has become one of my favorite brunch dishes now. It may be served, Western style, with a salad, French bread, and white wine, or it may be served Indian style, with a stack of *parathas* or toast, Tomato, Onion, and Green Coriander Relish (page 215), and steaming hot tea.

To make this omelette properly, it really helps to have a nonstick frying pan. The one I use measures 19 cm (7½ inches) across at the bottom, curving up to 25 cm (10 inches) across at the top. It is 5 cm (2 inches) in height. Your pan may have a somewhat different shape. It does not really matter. Just remember that the pie-shaped omelette rises slightly as it is cooking so a little space has to be left at the top. You also need a cover. If your frying pan does not have one, use aluminum foil.

Serves 4 to 6

450 g (1 lb) zucchinis

1¾ teaspoons salt, or to taste

5 tablespoons vegetable oil

1 large onion, peeled and
finely chopped

1 large or 2 small potatoes, peeled
and cut into 5 mm (¼ inch) dice

1–3 fresh, hot green chilies,
finely chopped

2 medium tomatoes, chopped

1½ teaspoons ground cumin

⅛–¼ teaspoon cayenne pepper (optional)

Freshly ground black pepper

9 large eggs

3 tablespoons finely chopped cilantro
(parsley may be substituted)

¼ teaspoon baking powder

Trim and discard the ends of the zucchinis and then grate them coarsely. Put the grated zucchinis in a bowl. Sprinkle ¾ teaspoon of the salt over them and mix thoroughly. Set aside for 30 minutes. Squeeze all the liquid out of the grated zucchinis and then separate the strands so they are no longer bunched up.

Put 3 tablespoons of the oil in a nonstick frying pan (see opposite) over medium heat. When hot, put in the onion. Stir and fry for a minute. Now put in the potatoes and the green chilies. Stir and fry for about 5 minutes or until the potato pieces are just about tender. Add the zucchinis, tomatoes, cumin, the remaining 1 teaspoon salt, cayenne, if using, and a generous amount of black pepper. Stir and cook for 2–3 minutes or until the tomato pieces are soft.

Set aside to cool.

Break the eggs into a bowl and beat well. Empty the cooled vegetable mixture into the beaten eggs and add the cilantro or parsley. Stir to mix. Sprinkle in the baking powder, making sure that it is lump-free. Mix again.

Wipe out the frying pan with a piece of paper towel. Pour in the remaining 2 tablespoons oil and set over low heat. When hot, pour in the egg mixture. Cover and cook on low heat for 15 minutes. Remove the cover. Now you have to turn the omelette over. Do it this way: Place a large plate over the frying pan. Put one hand on the plate. Quickly and deftly, lift the frying pan up with the other hand and turn it upside down over the plate. Your omelette will now be in the plate with its browned side on top. Slip it back into the frying pan and cook it, uncovered, for 5 minutes. Invert the omelette once again onto a serving platter. The lighter side should now be on the top.

Serve hot, warm, or at room temperature.

hard-boiled eggs in a spicy cream sauce

Malaidar unday

This delicious egg dish can be put together rather quickly and is just perfect for brunches, light lunches, and suppers. You could serve toast on the side or, if you like, rice and a crisp salad. If you prefer to serve a more traditional Indian meal, then *parathas* or Spiced Basmati Rice (page 194) and Gujerati-style Green Beans (page 131) would be suitable accompaniments.

This recipe calls for a small amount of chicken stock. If you have some homemade stock handy, well and good. Otherwise, use stock made with a cube, but adjust your salt as cube stock can be salty.

Serves 3 to 4

3 tablespoons vegetable oil

1 small onion, peeled and finely chopped

2.5 cm (1 inch) cube fresh ginger, peeled and finely grated

½ –1 fresh, hot green chili, finely chopped

300 ml (10 fl oz) light cream

1 tablespoon lemon juice

1 teaspoon ground, roasted cumin seeds (page 20)

⅛ teaspoon cayenne pepper

½ teaspoon salt

¼ teaspoon *garam masala* (page 21)

2 teaspoons tomato purée

150 ml (⅔ cup) chicken stock

6–8 hard-boiled eggs, peeled and cut crosswise into halves

1 tablespoon finely chopped cilantro or parsley (optional)

Put the oil in a large, preferably nonstick, frying pan and set over medium heat. When hot, put in the onion. Stir and fry the onion for about 3 minutes or until the pieces are browned at the edges. Put in the ginger and chili. Stir and fry for a minute. Now put in the cream, lemon juice, ground, roasted cumin seeds, cayenne, salt, *garam masala,* tomato purée, and chicken stock. Stir to mix thoroughly and bring to a simmer.

Put all the egg halves into the sauce in a single layer, cut side up. Spoon the sauce over them. Cook over medium heat for about 5 minutes, spooning the sauce frequently over the eggs as you do so. By this time the sauce will have become fairly thick. Put the egg halves carefully in a serving dish, cut side up, and pour the sauce over them. Garnish with cilantro or parsley, if you wish, sprinkling it lightly over the top.

vinegared eggs

Baida vindaloo

This vinegary, hard-boiled egg dish is almost like a pickle and perfect for taking out on picnics. It is, like all Goan-style *vindaloo* dishes, tart, hot, garlicky, and just very slightly sweet. I have lessened the tartness somewhat by cooking the eggs in a mixture of vinegar and water instead of just vinegar. Use the mildest vinegar that you can find. In this recipe, you may use anywhere from six to eight eggs without having to alter any of the other ingredients.

You could serve this dish with rice or an Indian bread. Cauliflower with Potatoes (page 144) would make a nice accompaniment.

Serves 3 to 4

4 cloves garlic, peeled

2.5 cm (1 inch) cube fresh ginger, peeled and very finely grated

$1/8 – 1/2$ teaspoon cayenne pepper

2 teaspoons paprika

$1 1/2$ teaspoons ground cumin

$1 1/4$ teaspoons salt

$1 1/2$ tablespoons brown sugar

2 tablespoons plus 150 ml ($1/2$ cup) mild white vinegar

3 tablespoons vegetable oil

2.5 cm (1 inch) cinnamon stick

3 small onions, peeled and finely chopped

$1/2$ teaspoon *garam masala* (page 21)

175 ml ($2/3$ cup) water

6–8 hard-boiled eggs, peeled and cut crosswise into halves

Mash the garlic cloves to a pulp or put them through a garlic press.

Combine the garlic, ginger, cayenne, paprika, cumin, salt, brown sugar, and 2 tablespoons vinegar in a cup or small bowl. Mix well.

Put the oil in a medium-sized frying pan and set over medium heat. When hot, put in the cinnamon stick. Let it sizzle for a few seconds. Now put in all the onions. Stir and fry for about 5 minutes or until the onions have softened. Put in the paste from the cup as well as the *garam masala*. Stir and fry for 2 minutes. Add 150 ml ($1/2$ cup) vinegar and 175 ml ($2/3$ cup) water. Stir to mix and bring to a simmer. Put all the egg halves into the frying pan in a single layer, cut side up, and spoon the sauce over them. Cook on medium heat for about 5 minutes or until the sauce has thickened. Spoon the sauce frequently over the eggs as you do so.

hard-boiled eggs cooked with potatoes

Unday aur aloo

This simple dish is quite a family favorite. We eat it with an Indian bread or plain rice. It makes a pleasant change from meat, and is economical too.

Serves 2 to 4

2 cloves garlic, peeled

2.5 cm (1 inch) cube fresh ginger, peeled and coarsely chopped

2 tablespoons plus 300 ml (1¼ cups) water

450 g (1 lb) potatoes (about 4 medium), peeled

6 tablespoons vegetable oil

2 small onions, peeled and finely chopped

⅛ teaspoon cayenne pepper

1 tablespoon ground coriander

1 teaspoon plain flour

4 tablespoons plain yogurt

3 medium tomatoes, peeled (page 30) and finely chopped

1½ teaspoons salt

½ teaspoon *garam masala* (page 21)

1 tablespoon very finely chopped cilantro (parsley may be substituted)

4 hard-boiled eggs, peeled

Put the garlic, ginger, and 2 tablespoons water into the container of a food processor or blender and blend until you have a paste.

Cut the potatoes into 1 cm (½ inch) thick slices. Now cut the slices lengthwise into 1 cm (½ inch) wide chips.

Put the oil in a large, preferably nonstick, frying pan and place over medium-high heat. When hot, put in the potatoes. Turn and fry them until all sides turn golden brown. The potatoes should not cook through. Remove them with a slotted spoon and put aside on a plate.

Put the onions into the same oil. Stir and fry until they turn medium brown. Now put in the garlic-ginger paste. Stir and fry for a minute. Put in the cayenne, ground coriander, and flour. Stir for a minute. Put in 1 tablespoon of the yogurt. Stir for about 30 seconds or until it has been incorporated into the sauce. Add all the yogurt this way, 1 tablespoon at a time. Now put in the tomatoes. Stir and fry for 2 minutes. Add 300 ml (1¼ cups) water and the salt. Bring to a boil. Cover the frying pan, turn the heat to low, and simmer for 10 minutes.

Put the potatoes into the sauce and bring to a simmer. Cover, turn heat to low and simmer for 10 minutes or until the potatoes are just tender. Add the *garam masala* and cilantro or parsley. Stir gently to mix.

Halve the eggs, crosswise, and carefully put them into the frying pan with the cut sides up. Try not to let the yolks fall out. Spoon some sauce over the eggs. Bring to a simmer. Cover and simmer on low heat for 5 minutes.

There is nothing quite like good fresh fish. It is light, cooks fast, and may be prepared simply and elegantly at the same time. Needless to say, the types of fish available in Indian rivers, lakes, and seas are different from the ones found in the colder northern waters.

What I have done for this chapter is to work out Indian-style recipes for the fish that are commonly available in the West. The shrimp I have used are the cooked, packed frozen ones that are found in supermarkets and fish markets. Just look for the largest and best varieties that you can find.

Indians eat a fair amount of breaded, fried fish. I have used plaice (a type of flounder) for this as it is similar to our *pomfret*, at least in general shape. Our mackerel has a plumper form but is very similar in taste. So I have used it for a west coast recipe that calls for a fresh coriander and lemon marinade. We have no cod, halibut, or haddock in India but they are similar in texture to some of our river fish. I have used them in Indian-style recipes in which they are cooked with tomatoes or yogurt or cauliflower.

I have even included a recipe for mussels. This is a Goan recipe, one of the few in this book that uses fresh coconut. It is an exquisite dish.

I need hardly repeat that if you are buying fresh fish, make sure that it is fresh. The gills should be bright red, the eyes clear, the skin shiny, and the body firm and taut. The fish should not have a pronounced fishy odor.

fish

goan-style mussels
Thisra

Although they are eaten with rice in Goa, I love to serve these mussels all by themselves as a first course.

Serves 6

30–36 small to medium-sized mussels

2.5 cm (1 inch) cube fresh ginger, peeled and coarsely chopped

8 cloves garlic, peeled

370 ml (1$^1/_2$ cups) water

4 tablespoons vegetable oil

2 medium onions, peeled and chopped

1$^1/_2$–2 fresh, hot green chilies, sliced into fine rounds

$^1/_2$ teaspoon ground turmeric

2 teaspoons ground cumin

$^1/_2$ fresh coconut, finely grated (page 18)

$^1/_2$ teaspoon salt

Wash and scrub the mussels well, removing the beards that are often attached to them. Discard any shells that are open.

Put the ginger and garlic into the container of an electric blender or food processor. Add 120 ml ($^1/_2$ cup) water and blend until fairly smooth.

Put the oil in a large frying pan and set over medium heat. When hot, put in the onions and sauté them until they turn translucent. Now put in the paste from the blender, green chilies, turmeric, and cumin. Stir and fry for a minute. Add the coconut, salt, and 250 ml (1 cup) water. Bring to a boil. (This much of the recipe may be made several hours ahead of time.) Add the mussels. Mix well and bring to a boil. Cover tightly. Lower heat slightly and let the mussels steam for 6–10 minutes or until they open up. Discard any mussels that fail to open. Serve immediately.

shrimp with zucchinis

Jhinga aur ghia

We do not have zucchinis in India but we do have a variety of similar squashes that are often cooked with shrimp and other seafood. Here is one such combination. I prefer to use relatively small zucchinis weighing about 100 g ($^1/_4$ lb) each. If you can get only larger ones, just cut them appropriately so that each piece is just a little larger than a shrimp.

I like to serve these shrimp with Spiced Basmati Rice (page 194) or Plain Long-grain Rice (page 192) and Red Split Lentils with Cumin Seeds (page 165).

Serves 4

350 g ($^3/_4$ lb) zucchinis (see above)

1$^1/_4$ teaspoons salt

350 g ($^3/_4$ lb) peeled, good-quality frozen shrimp, defrosted and patted dry

5 tablespoons vegetable oil

6 cloves garlic, peeled and very finely chopped

75 g (1 cup) finely chopped cilantro (weight without lower stems and roots)

1 fresh, hot green chili, finely chopped

$^1/_2$ teaspoon ground turmeric

1$^1/_2$ teaspoons ground cumin

$^1/_4$ teaspoon cayenne pepper

3 small canned tomatoes, finely chopped, plus 120 ml ($^1/_2$ cup) liquid from can

1 teaspoon peeled, very finely grated fresh ginger

1 tablespoon lemon juice

Scrub the zucchinis and trim them. Now cut them in 4 slices lengthwise. Cut each slice, lengthwise, into 4 long strips. Cut the strips into thirds, crosswise. Put the zucchinis in a bowl. Sprinkle $^1/_4$ teaspoon of the salt over the pieces. Toss to mix and set aside for 30–40 minutes. Drain and pat dry.

Put the shrimp on paper towels and dry them off as well.

Put the oil in a wide pan or frying pan and set over medium-high heat. When hot, put in the chopped garlic. Stir and fry until the garlic pieces turn a medium-brown color. Put in the zucchinis, cilantro, green chili, turmeric, cumin, cayenne, tomatoes and their liquid, ginger, lemon juice, and remaining 1 teaspoon salt. Stir to mix and bring to a simmer. Add the shrimp and stir them in. Cover, turn heat to low, and simmer for 3 minutes.

Uncover, turn the heat to medium and boil away the liquid, if there is any, so that you are left with a thick sauce.

shrimp in a dark sauce

Rasedar jhinga

Serve this with Plain Basmati Rice (page 193), Cauliflower with Potatoes (page 144), and Tomato, Onion, and Cilantro Relish (page 215).

Serves 4

1 medium onion, peeled and coarsely chopped

5 cloves garlic, peeled

2.5 cm (1 inch) cube fresh ginger, peeled and coarsely chopped

3 tablespoons plus 300 ml (1¼ cups) water

4 tablespoons vegetable oil

2.5 cm (1 inch) cinnamon stick

6 cardamom pods

2 bay leaves

2 teaspoons ground cumin

1 teaspoon ground coriander

2 medium tomatoes, peeled (page 30) and very finely chopped

5 tablespoons plain yogurt

½ teaspoon ground turmeric

¼ –½ teaspoon cayenne pepper

About ¾ teaspoon salt

350 g (¾ lb) peeled, good-quality frozen shrimp, defrosted and patted dry

¼ teaspoon *garam masala* (page 21)

2 tablespoons finely chopped cilantro

Blend the onion, garlic, ginger, and 3 tablespoons water in an electric blender until you have a paste.

Put the oil in a 20–23 cm (8–9 inch) wide frying pan and set over medium-high heat. When hot, put in the cinnamon, cardamom pods, and bay leaves. Stir for 3–4 seconds. Put in the paste from the blender. Stir and fry for about 5 minutes or until the paste turns a light brown color. Add the cumin and ground coriander. Stir and fry for 30 seconds. Put in the tomatoes. Stir and keep frying until the paste has a nice reddish brown look to it. Now put in 1 tablespoon of the yogurt. Stir and fry for 10–15 seconds or until it is incorporated in the sauce. Add all the yogurt this way. Add the turmeric and cayenne and stir for a minute. Put in 300 ml (1¼ cups) water, the salt, and the shrimp. Stir to mix and bring to a boil over medium-high heat. Stir and cook for about 5 minutes or until you have a thick sauce. Do not overcook. Sprinkle with the *garam masala* and mix. Garnish with cilantro.

halibut with cauliflower

Macchi aur phool gobi

All you need to serve with this dish is some rice and a relish.

Serves 4 to 6

2.5 cm (1 inch) thick halibut steak, weighing about 900 g (2 lb); 2 smaller steaks of equal thickness will do

1½ teaspoons ground cumin

1½ teaspoons ground coriander

½ teaspoon ground turmeric

About ½ teaspoon cayenne pepper

1½ teaspoons salt

1 large onion, peeled and coarsely chopped

Two 2.5 cm (1 inch) cubes fresh ginger, peeled and coarsely chopped

1–2 fresh, hot green chilies, roughly cut into 3–4 pieces each

3 tablespoons plus 450 ml (2 cups) water

7 tablespoons vegetable oil

350 g (¾ lb) florets from a cauliflower head, each about 5 cm (2 inches) in length and about 2.5 cm (1 inch) across at the top

Freshly ground black pepper

6 tablespoons plain yogurt

Have the fish store cut the halibut steak into pieces approximately 5 x 4 x 2.5 cm (2 x 1½ x 1 inches). Or do this at home with a heavy cleaver that can hack through the bone. Leave the skin on.

Put the fish pieces in a bowl. Sprinkle ½ teaspoon of the cumin, ½ teaspoon of the coriander, ¼ teaspoon of the turmeric, ¼ teaspoon of the cayenne, and ½ teaspoon of the salt over them. Toss to mix evenly. Set aside for ½–1 hour.

Put the onion, ginger, green chilies, and 3 tablespoons water into the container of an electric blender. Blend until you have a paste.

Heat 6 tablespoons of the oil in a 30 cm (12 inch), preferably nonstick, sauté pan or deep frying pan over medium heat. When hot, put in the cauliflower florets. Stir and fry them until they are very lightly browned. Remove with a slotted spoon and set aside in a bowl. Sprinkle ¼ teaspoon of the salt and some black pepper over the cauliflower. Toss to mix.

Put the fish pieces into the same pan in a single layer and brown lightly on both sides. Do not let the fish cook through. Remove the fish pieces carefully and put on a plate.

Add another tablespoon of oil to the pan and set over medium-high heat. When hot, put in the paste from the blender. Stir and fry the paste until it turns a light brown color. Now add the remaining 1 teaspoon cumin, 1 teaspoon coriander, ⅛–¼ teaspoon cayenne, and ¾ teaspoon salt. Stir and fry for a minute. Put in 1 tablespoon of the yogurt. Stir and fry it for about 30 seconds or until it is incorporated into the paste. Add all the yogurt this way, 1 tablespoon at a time. Now pour in 450 ml (2 cups) water, stir, and bring to a simmer. Simmer on medium heat for 2 minutes. Gently put in the fish pieces and the cauliflower. Cover partially and cook on medium heat for about 5 minutes or until the fish is cooked through and the cauliflower is tender, spooning the sauce over the fish and vegetables several times.

fried flounder fillets

Tali hui macchi

This is one of the simpler fish dishes served in many parts of India, with each area using its own local fish. The breading is, of course, a Western influence. Wedges of lemon or some tomato ketchup may be served on the side.

Serves 4

700 g (1½ lb) flounder fillets with dark skin removed

¾ teaspoon salt

Freshly ground black pepper

1½ teaspoons ground cumin

½ teaspoon ground turmeric

½ teaspoon cayenne pepper

2 tablespoons very finely chopped cilantro (parsley may be substituted)

2 large eggs

4 teaspoons water

175 g (1 cup) fresh breadcrumbs

Vegetable oil for sautéing (enough to have 1 cm/½ inch in frying pan)

Cut the fish fillets, crosswise and at a slight diagonal, into 2 cm (¾ inch) wide strips. Lay the strips on a plate and sprinkle both sides with the salt, black pepper, cumin, turmeric, cayenne, and cilantro or parsley. Pat down the spices. Set aside for 15 minutes.

Break the eggs into a deep plate. Add 4 teaspoons water and beat lightly. Spread the breadcrumbs on a plate. Dip the fish in the egg and then in the crumbs to coat evenly.

Put about 1 cm (½ inch) oil in a large frying pan and set over a medium heat. When hot, put in as many pieces of fish as the pan will hold easily. Fry for 2–3 minutes on each side or until golden brown. Drain on paper towels. Fry all the fish strips this way and serve hot.

cod steaks in a spicy tomato sauce

Timatar wali macchi

I like to serve this with Rice and Peas (page 196) and Spinach Cooked with Onions (page 156).

Serves 4

4 cod steaks, weighing about 900 g (2 lb)

1¼ teaspoons salt

½ teaspoon cayenne pepper

¼ teaspoon ground turmeric

9 tablespoons vegetable oil

1 teaspoon fennel seeds

1 teaspoon mustard seeds

2 medium onions, peeled and finely chopped

2 cloves garlic, peeled and finely chopped

2 teaspoons ground cumin

One 450 g (1 lb) can of tomatoes, with the tomatoes chopped up

½ teaspoon ground, roasted cumin seeds (page 20), optional

¼ teaspoon *garam masala* (page 21)

Pat the fish steaks dry with paper towels. Rub them, on both sides, with ¼ teaspoon of the salt, ¼ teaspoon of the cayenne, and the turmeric. Set aside for 30 minutes.

Put 4 tablespoons of the oil in a saucepan and set over medium heat. When hot, put in the fennel and mustard seeds. As soon as the mustard seeds begin to pop – this just takes a few seconds – put in the onions and garlic. Stir and fry until the onions turn slightly brown. Now put in the cumin, 1 teaspoon salt, and ¼ teaspoon cayenne. Stir once and put in the tomatoes and their liquid, the ground, roasted cumin seeds, if using, and the *garam masala*. Bring to a boil. Cover, turn heat to low, and simmer gently for 15 minutes.

Meanwhile, preheat the oven to 180°C/350°F.

Put the remaining 5 tablespoons of the oil in a large, preferably nonstick, frying pan and set over medium-high heat. When hot, put in the fish steaks and brown on both sides. Do not cook the fish through. Put the steaks in a baking dish. Pour the cooked tomato sauce over the fish and bake, uncovered, for 15 minutes or until the fish is done.

salmon steamed with crushed mustard seeds and tomato

Salmon bhapey

Steaming fish that has first been rubbed with a paste of crushed mustard seeds, turmeric, chili powder, and mustard oil is typical of Bengali cooking. I have changed the fish from the more commonly used mackerel-like *hilsa* to salmon (you could also use haddock). I have also added cumin and tomato to complement the slight oiliness of the salmon. Serve with plain rice, a green vegetable, and a dried bean dish. Mustard oil is wonderfully zesty. Pungent when raw, it turns sweet when heated. If you cannot find it, use a good, extra-virgin olive oil. Its taste is different but its intensity is the same. Good-quality fish is essential.

You may use one of two methods for steaming:

1. Put the bowl of diced salmon into a large pot. Pour boiling water into the pot so that it comes one-third of the way up the sides of the bowl. Cover the pot and steam.

2. Put water in the bottom third of a large wok. Bring to a boil. Put a bamboo steaming tray or a perforated metal steaming tray on top of the water. Place the bowl of salmon on the tray, cover the wok, and steam.

Serves 4

550 g (1¼ lb) thick salmon fillet from the center of the fish, skinned

2 teaspoons black mustard seeds

½–1 fresh, hot green chili, finely chopped

½ teaspoon ground cumin

¼ teaspoon ground turmeric

¾ teaspoon salt

Freshly ground black pepper

½ teaspoon cayenne pepper

½ large very ripe tomato, peeled (page 30) and finely chopped

3 tablespoons mustard oil

1 tablespoon water

Cut the fish fillet into 2.5 cm (1 inch) squares. Grind the mustard seeds coarsely in a clean coffee grinder or other spice grinder.

In a shallow bowl large enough to hold the fish, combine the mustard seeds, green chili, cumin, turmeric, salt, black pepper, cayenne, tomato, and mustard oil. Mix well. Add the water and mix. Add the fish and mix gently. Cover with a plate or aluminum foil and set aside for 10 minutes.

Place the covered bowl in the steaming utensil, cover the utensil, and steam gently for 10 minutes. Remove the bowl, toss its contents gently to mix, then cover the bowl and put it back in the utensil. Cover the utensil and steam for 10–15 minutes or until the fish pieces are opaque.

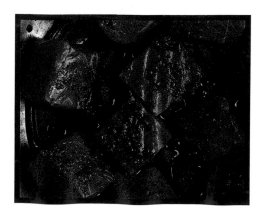

haddock baked in a yogurt sauce

Dahi wali macchi

This is one of my favorite fish dishes — and it is so easy to put together. All you have to do is combine the ingredients in a baking dish and bake for about 30 minutes. You do have to boil down the sauce later but that takes just an additional 5 minutes. I like to serve this dish with Mushroom *Pullao* (page 199) and Frozen Spinach with Potatoes (page 157). If you cannot get haddock, use any other thick-cut fish such as cod or halibut.

Serves 4 to 6

2 medium onions, peeled

900 g (2 lb) 2.5 cm (1 inch) thick fresh haddock fillets

450 ml (2 cups) plain yogurt

2 tablespoons lemon juice

1 teaspoon sugar

1$\frac{1}{2}$ teaspoons salt

$\frac{1}{4}$ teaspoon coarsely ground black pepper

2 teaspoons ground cumin

2 tablespoons ground coriander

$\frac{1}{4}$ teaspoon *garam masala* (page 21)

$\frac{1}{2}$ –$\frac{3}{4}$ teaspoon cayenne pepper

1 teaspoon peeled, finely grated fresh ginger

3 tablespoons vegetable oil

3 tablespoons unsalted cold butter, cut into pats

Preheat the oven to 190°C/350°F.

Cut the onions into 3 mm ($\frac{1}{8}$ inch) thick slices and line a large baking dish with them. (The dish should be large enough to hold the fish in a single layer. It need not be more than 4 cm (1$\frac{1}{2}$ inches) in depth.) Cut the fish fillets, crosswise, into 7.5 cm (3 inch) long segments and lay them over the onions.

Put the yogurt into a bowl. Beat it lightly. Add the lemon juice, sugar, salt, black pepper, cumin, coriander, *garam masala*, cayenne, and ginger. Mix well. Add the oil and mix again. Pour this sauce over the fish, making sure some of it goes under the pieces. Cover (with aluminum foil, if necessary) and bake in the upper third of the oven for 30 minutes or until the fish is just done.

Carefully, pour out all the liquid from the baking dish into a small saucepan. (Keep the fish covered and in a warm place.) The sauce will look thin and "separated." Bring it to a boil. Boil rapidly until there is about 350 ml (1$\frac{1}{2}$ cups) of sauce left. Take the saucepan off the heat. Put in the butter and beat in with a fork. As soon as it has melted, pour the sauce over the fish and serve.

Note: You may also serve the dish cold, after it has been refrigerated overnight, with a green salad.

grilled mackerel with lemon and cilantro

Hare masale mali macchi

Indian mackerel seem to me to be much plumper than other mackerel. Perhaps the warmer waters make them lazier. Goan fishermen on India's west coast roast them right on the beach over smoldering rice straws. The blackened skin is then peeled away and the now pristine, skinless fish served with a simple vinegar dressing. A good fresh mackerel needs nothing more.

Further up the same coast, in large cities like Bombay, the fish is marinated first in a dressing of lemon juice and cilantro and then fried or grilled. Here is the Bombay recipe. I often serve it with Mushroom *Pullao* (page 199) and Cabbage with Peas (page 140).

Serves 2

2 medium-sized, whole mackerel, about 750 g (1½ lb) in all, cleaned

3 tablespoons very finely chopped cilantro

½–1 fresh, hot green chili, finely chopped

1 tablespoon lemon juice

½ teaspoon salt

Freshly ground black pepper

4 tablespoons unsalted butter, cut into pats

Cut the heads off the mackerel. Split them all the way down the stomach and then lay them out flat, skinside up, on a firm surface.

Now bone the fish this way: Press down firmly with the heel of your hand all along the backbone. This should loosen the bone from the flesh somewhat. Now turn the fish over so the skinside is down. Work your fingers (or else use a knife) under the bones to prise them away from the fish.

Cut 2–3 shallow diagonal slashes on the skinside of each fish.

Combine the cilantro, green chili, lemon juice, salt, and black pepper in a bowl. Mix well. Rub this mixture all over the fish. Set aside for 45 minutes.

Heat the grill. Put the fish in the grill pan, with the rack removed, skinside up, and dot with half the butter. Grill, 10 cm (4 inches) away from the heat, for about 5 minutes. Turn the fish over, dot with the remaining butter, and grill for 4 minutes or until golden brown.

love all vegetables — from shiny purple eggplants that can be fried very simply with a light dusting of turmeric and cayenne to the humble potato that, in India, is cooked in at least a thousand different ways including one in which black pepper is the main seasoning.

As many Indians are vegetarians, we have, over the years, worked out a great variety of ways to cook our everyday vegetables such as cabbages, green beans, beets, and carrots. Sometimes the vegetables are cut into shreds or slices and quickly stir-fried with whole spices such as cumin seeds and mustard seeds. These are referred to as "dry" vegetables and rarely have even the glimmer of a sauce. At other times we may cook root vegetables in a thick ginger-garlic sauce or with tomatoes. Such dishes are referred to as "wet" dishes because of the sauce. They are generally served in small, individual bowls. Both "dry" and "wet" dishes may be served with rice or Indian breads.

For those of you who are vegetarians — or want to cut down on your meat intake — you can make perfectly balanced meals by picking two or three vegetables from this chapter and then adding a pulse dish, a rice or bread, and a yogurt relish.

vegetables

gujerati-style green beans

Gujerati sem

Here is a very simple yet delicious way to cook green beans. This dish goes well both with Indian meals and with grilled and roast meats (I like it with sausages). Gujeratis often cook green vegetables with a little baking soda in order to preserve their bright color. I am told that this kills the vitamins. So I blanch the beans and rinse them out quickly under cold, running water instead. This works equally well. I generally do the blanching and rinsing ahead of time and do the final cooking just before we sit down to eat.

If you do not want the beans to be hot, either do without the red chili or else discard all its seeds and use just the skin for flavor.

Serves 4

450 g (1 lb) fresh green French beans

4 tablespoons vegetable oil

1 tablespoon black mustard seeds

4 cloves garlic, peeled and very finely chopped

$^1/_2$–1 hot, dried red chili, coarsely crushed in a mortar

1 teaspoon salt

$^1/_2$ teaspoon sugar

Freshly ground black pepper

Trim the beans and cut them into 2.5 cm (1 inch) lengths. Blanch the beans by dropping them into a pot of boiling water and boiling rapidly for 3–4 minutes or until they are just tender. Drain immediately in a colander and rinse under cold, running water. Set aside.

Put the oil in a large frying pan and set over medium heat. When hot, put in the mustard seeds. As soon as the mustard seeds begin to pop, put in the garlic. Stir the garlic pieces until they turn light brown. Put in the crushed red chili and stir for a few seconds. Put in the green beans, salt, and sugar. Stir to mix. Turn the heat to medium low. Stir and cook the beans for 7–8 minutes or until they have absorbed the flavor of the spices. Add the black pepper, mix, and serve.

spicy green beans

Masaledar sem

These green beans may, of course, be served with an Indian dinner. But they could perk up a simple meal of roast chicken, pork chops, or meat loaf as well. They are tart and hot and would complement the plainest of everyday foods with their zesty blend of flavors. Another good thing about them — they may be made ahead of time and reheated.

Serves 6

750 g (1½ lb) fresh green French beans

Piece fresh ginger, about 4 cm (1½ inches) long and 2.5 cm (1 inch) thick, peeled and coarsely chopped

10 cloves garlic, peeled

350 ml (1½ cups) water

5 tablespoons vegetable oil

2 teaspoons cumin seeds

1 dried, hot red chili, lightly crushed in a mortar

2 teaspoons ground coriander

2 medium tomatoes, peeled (page 30) and finely chopped

About 1¼ teaspoons salt

3 tablespoons lemon juice, or to taste

1 teaspoon ground, roasted cumin seeds (page 20)

Freshly ground black pepper

Trim the green beans and cut them, crosswise, at 5 mm (¼ inch) intervals. Put the ginger and garlic into the container of an electric blender or food processor. Add 120 ml (½ cup) of the measured water and blend until fairly smooth.

Put the oil in a wide, heavy pot and set over medium heat. When hot, put in the cumin seeds. Five seconds later, put in the crushed chili. As soon as it darkens, pour in the ginger-garlic paste. Stir and cook for about a minute. Put in the coriander. Stir a few times. Now put in the chopped tomatoes. Stir and cook for about 2 minutes, mashing up the tomato pieces with the back of a slotted spoon as you do so. Put in the beans, salt, and the remaining water. Bring to a simmer. Cover, turn heat to low, and cook for 8–10 minutes or until the beans are tender. Remove the cover. Add the lemon juice, ground, roasted cumin seeds, and a generous amount of freshly ground black pepper.

Turn up heat and boil away all of the liquid, stirring the beans gently as you do so.

green beans with ginger and cilantro

Hare masale ki sem

You may serve these tangy, ginger- and green-coriander-flavored green beans
with almost any Indian meal or with roast leg of lamb, roast chicken, or even sausages.
Cold leftovers may be tossed into a green salad.
The green beans should, ideally, be cut crosswise into 5 mm (¼ inch) segments.
However, if you are feeling lazy, as I often do, you may cut them into 1 cm (½ inch) or
2.5 cm (1 inch) lengths. Just cut them evenly, whatever length you choose.

Serves 4 to 5

550 g (1¼ lb) fresh green beans

2.5 cm (1 inch) piece fresh ginger, peeled
and very thinly sliced

4 tablespoons vegetable oil

½ teaspoon black mustard seeds

2 teaspoons ground cumin

¼ teaspoon ground turmeric

¾ teaspoon salt, or to taste

1 fresh, hot green chili, finely chopped

4 teaspoons lemon juice

150 ml (5 oz) chicken stock or water

5–6 tablespoons finely chopped cilantro

Trim the green beans and cut them, crosswise, into 2.5 cm (1 inch) segments (see above).

Stack a few ginger slices together at a time and cut them into very fine strips.

Put the oil in a large frying pan or wok and set over medium-high heat. When hot, put in the mustard seeds. As soon as the mustard seeds begin to pop — this takes just a few seconds — put in the ginger strips. Stir and fry until the ginger starts to brown, a matter of a few seconds. Put in the green beans and toss once or twice. Now put in the cumin, turmeric, salt, and green chili. Toss once or twice. Add the lemon juice and chicken stock or water. Stir and bring to a simmer. Cover, turn heat to low, and simmer gently for 10 minutes or until the beans are almost tender. Add the cilantro, toss, and cover again for a minute. Uncover, toss, and boil away all liquid (if any is left) at a higher heat.

fried eggplant slices

Tala hua baigan

This is one of the simplest ways of cooking eggplant in India. Ideally, the frying should be done at the very last minute and the melt-in-the-mouth slices served as soon as they come out of the hot oil. Sometimes I arrange these slices, like petals, around a roast leg of lamb. They can, of course, be served with any Indian meal.

Leftover eggplant slices, if there are any, may be heated together with any leftover, Indian-style meat the following day. The combination makes for a very good new dish.

Serves 4 to 6

550 g (1¼ lb) (1 medium) eggplant
About 1 teaspoon salt
½ teaspoon ground turmeric
⅛–½ teaspoon cayenne pepper
Some freshly ground black pepper
Vegetable oil for sautéing
6–8 lemon wedges

Cut the eggplant into quarters, lengthwise, and then cut, crosswise, into 1 cm (½ inch) thick wedges.

Mix the salt, turmeric, cayenne, and black pepper in a small bowl. Sprinkle this combination over the eggplant wedges and mix well.

Put about 1 cm (⅓ inch) oil in a 20–23 cm (8–9 inch) frying pan and set over medium heat. When hot, put in as many eggplant slices as the pan will hold in a single layer. Fry until reddish gold on one side. Turn the slices and fry them on their reverse side. Remove with a slotted spoon and spread out on a plate lined with paper towels.

Do a second batch, adding more oil, if you need to.

Serve with lemon wedges.

the lake palace hotel's eggplant cooked in the pickling style

Baigan achari

Right in the center of a lake in the former royal city of Udaipur is a summer palace, now converted, as most Indian palaces seem fated to be, into a spectacular hotel. This recipe comes from its master chef, Shankerlal, and in its finished effect is not unlike a spicy ratatouille. It is an exquisite dish. While *kalonji* – black onion seeds – do give this dish its special "pickled" taste, you may use cumin seeds instead.

I love to eat this dish with a hearty lamb stew, such as *Rogan josh* (Red Lamb or Beef Stew, page 70) and a bread (such as *parathas*). If you do not feel like an all-Indian meal, you could serve it with a leg of roast lamb and plain rice. I think it also tastes excellent cold. I often dole out individual portions on lettuce leaves and serve them as a first course. Sometimes I serve this dish for lunch with cold chicken, cold lamb, or sliced ham.

Serves 6

2.5 cm (1 inch) cube fresh ginger, peeled and coarsely chopped

6 large cloves garlic, peeled

50 ml ($^1/_4$ cup) water

750 g (1$^3/_4$ lb) eggplant (1 large or 2 small)

About 350 ml (1$^1/_2$ cups) plus 3 tablespoons vegetable oil

1 teaspoon fennel seeds

$^1/_2$ teaspoon *kalonji* or cumin seeds

3 medium tomatoes, peeled (page 30) and finely chopped

1 tablespoon ground coriander

$^1/_4$ teaspoon ground turmeric

$^1/_3$ teaspoon cayenne pepper (more, if you like)

About 1$^1/_4$ teaspoons salt

Put the ginger and garlic into the container of an electric blender or food processor. Add the water and blend until fairly smooth.

Cut the eggplant into slices or wedges that are 2 cm ($^3/_4$ inch) thick and about 4–5 cm (1$^1/_2$–2 inches) long.

Set a strainer over a bowl.

Put 120 ml ($^1/_2$ cup) of the oil in a deep, 25–30 cm (10–12 inch) frying pan or saucepan and set over medium-high heat. When hot, put in as many eggplant slices as the pan will hold in a single layer. Let them turn a reddish brown color. Turn them over and brown the reverse sides. Remove the slices and put them in the strainer. Add another 120 ml ($^1/_2$ cup) of oil to the frying pan and heat it. Brown a second batch of eggplant slices, just as you did the first. You will probably need to do three batches, adding fresh oil to the frying pan each time. (You may now turn off the heat under the frying pan and let the eggplant drain for about an hour or you may proceed with the next step. The idea is to get rid of some of the oil. You will achieve this end either way, though I think it helps slightly to get rid of the oil at the earlier stage.)

Put 3 tablespoons oil in the frying pan and set over medium heat. When hot, put in the fennel seeds and *kalonji* or cumin seeds. As soon as the fennel seeds turn a few shades darker – this takes just a few seconds – put in the chopped tomatoes, the ginger-garlic mixture, coriander, turmeric, cayenne, and salt. Stir and cook for 5–6 minutes, breaking the tomato pieces with the back of a slotted spoon. Turn the heat up slightly and continue to stir and cook until the spice mixture gets thick and pastelike.

Now put in the fried eggplant slices and mix gently. Cook on medium-low heat for about 5 minutes, stirring very gently as you do so. Cover the pan, turn heat to very low, and cook another 5–10 minutes if you think it is necessary.

Oil will have collected at the bottom of the frying pan. Use a slotted spoon to lift the eggplant out of this oil when you serve.

You could also serve this dish cold, almost as if it were a salad. In that case, store it with all its oil in the refrigerator. Take it out of the oil only when you serve.

beets with onions

Shorvedar chukander

I love beets, in almost any form. Even people who do not have a weakness for this particular root vegetable, manage to succumb to the charms of this recipe. It is a kind of stew, thickened by the onions floating around in it and somewhat tart in flavor because of the tomatoes it contains. As there is a fair amount of sauce, I frequently serve it with Beef Baked with Yogurt and Black Pepper (page 69), a somewhat dry dish, and with Tomato, Onion, and Cilantro Relish (page 215). *Chapatis* are the ideal bread to serve with this meal, though plain rice would also taste good.

Serves 3 to 4

350 g ($^3/_4$ lb) raw beets
(weight without stems and leaves)

4 tablespoons vegetable oil

1 teaspoon cumin seeds

1 clove garlic, peeled and
very finely chopped

1 large onion, peeled and
coarsely chopped

1 teaspoon plain flour

$^1/_8$–$^1/_2$ teaspoon cayenne pepper

2 medium tomatoes, peeled (page 30)
and very finely chopped

1 teaspoon salt

300 ml (1$^1/_4$ cups) water

Peel the beets and cut them into wedges. A medium-sized beet, about 5 cm (2 inches) in length, should, for example, be cut into 6 wedges.

Put the oil in a medium-sized saucepan and set over medium heat. When hot, put in the cumin seeds. Let them sizzle for 5 seconds. Put in the garlic. Stir and fry until the garlic pieces turn golden. Put in the onion. Stir and fry for 2 minutes. Put in the flour and cayenne. Stir and fry for a minute. Now put in the beets, the tomatoes, salt, and water. Bring to a simmer. Cover, turn heat to low, and simmer for 30 minutes or until the beets are tender. Remove lid, turn up heat to medium, and cook uncovered for about 7 minutes or until the sauce has thickened slightly.

This dish may be made ahead of time and reheated.

cabbage with peas

Bund gobi aur matar

Here is a simple cabbage dish that you could serve just as easily with grilled pork chops as with an Indian meal.

Serves 4

450–550 g (1–1¼ lb) green cabbage

150 g (1¼ cups) frozen peas

5 tablespoons vegetable oil

2 teaspoons cumin seeds

2 bay leaves

¼ teaspoon ground turmeric

¼ teaspoon cayenne pepper

1 fresh, hot green chili, very finely chopped

¾ teaspoon salt

¾ teaspoon sugar

¼ teaspoon *garam masala* (page 21)

Core the cabbage and cut it into very fine, long shreds. Put the peas in a strainer and hold them under warm, running water until they separate.

Put the oil in a wide frying pan and set over medium-high heat. When hot, put in the cumin seeds and bay leaves. As soon as the bay leaves begin to take on color – this just takes a few seconds – put in the cabbage and peas and stir them for 30 seconds. Add the turmeric and cayenne. Stir to mix. Cover, turn heat to low, and cook for 5 minutes or until the vegetables are just tender. Add the green chili, salt, and sugar. Stir to mix. Cover and cook on low heat another 2–3 minutes. Remove cover and sprinkle in the *garam masala*. Stir gently and mix.

Note: Remove the bay leaves before serving – they are not meant to be eaten.

gujerati-style cabbage with carrots

Sambhara

This is the kind of everyday dish that is served in the state of Gujerat. It may be served as well with pork chops as with an Indian meal.

Serves 4 to 6

350 g ($^3/_4$ lb) green cabbage
350 g ($^3/_4$ lb) carrots
$^1/_2$–1 fresh, hot green chili
4 tablespoons vegetable oil
Pinch of ground asafetida (optional)
1 tablespoon black mustard seeds
1 dried, hot red chili
About 1$^1/_4$ teaspoons salt
$^1/_2$ teaspoon sugar
4 heaped tablespoons chopped cilantro
1 tablespoon lemon juice

Core the cabbage and cut it into fine, long shreds. Peel the carrots and grate them coarsely. Cut the green chili into thin, long strips.

Put the oil in a wide, deep pot and set over medium-high heat. When hot, put in the asafetida, if using. A second later, put in the mustard seeds. As soon as the mustard seeds begin to pop – this takes just a few seconds – put in the red chili. Stir once. The chili should turn dark red in seconds. Now put in the cabbage, carrots, and green chili. Turn the heat down to medium and stir the vegetables for half a minute. Add the salt, sugar, and cilantro. Stir and cook for another 5 minutes or until the vegetables are just done and retain some of their crispness. Add the lemon juice. Stir to mix.

Note: Remove the whole red chili before serving.

cauliflower with onion and tomato

Phool gobi ki bhaji

A good all-round vegetable dish that goes well with most Indian meat dishes.

Serves 6

Two medium-sized cauliflowers, about 1 kg (2¼ lb) in all (you need about 725 g/1 lb 10 oz florets)

1 medium onion, peeled and coarsely chopped

Two 2.5 cm (1 inch) cubes fresh ginger, peeled and coarsely chopped

About 7 tablespoons water

5 tablespoons vegetable oil

6 cloves garlic, peeled and very finely chopped

1 teaspoon ground cumin

1 teaspoon ground coriander

2 small tomatoes, peeled (page 30) and finely chopped

½ teaspoon ground turmeric

¼ –½ teaspoon cayenne pepper

½ –1 fresh, hot green chili, finely chopped

1 tablespoon lemon juice

1¾ teaspoons salt

¼ teaspoon *garam masala* (page 21)

Break up the cauliflower into florets that are about 4 cm (1½ inches) across at the head and 4–5 cm (1½ –2 inches) in length.

Let them soak in a bowl of water for 30 minutes. Drain.

Put the onion and ginger into the container of an electric blender along with 4 tablespoons of the water. Blend until you have a paste.

Put the oil in a 23–25 cm (9–10 inch) wide pot or deep frying pan and set over medium-high heat. When hot, put in the garlic. Stir and fry until the pieces turn a medium-brown color. Put in the cauliflower. Stir and fry for about 2 minutes or until the cauliflower pieces pick up a few brown spots. Remove the cauliflower with a slotted spoon and put in a bowl. Put the onion-ginger mixture into the same pan. Stir and fry it for a minute. Now put in the cumin, coriander, and tomatoes. Stir and fry this mixture until it turns a medium-brown color. If it starts to burn, turn the heat down slightly and sprinkle in a tablespoon of water. Then keep frying until you have the right color. Add the turmeric, cayenne, green chili, lemon juice, and salt. Give a few good stirs and turn heat to low. Now put in the cauliflower and any possible liquid in the cauliflower bowl. Stir gently to mix. Add 3 tablespoons of the water, stir again, and bring to a simmer. Cover and cook on gentle heat, stirring now and then, for 5–10 minutes or until the cauliflower is just done. Remove lid and sprinkle *garam masala* over the top. Stir to mix.

cauliflower with potatoes

Phool gobi aur aloo ki bhaji

This is the kind of comforting "homey" dish that most North Indians enjoy. It has no sauce and is generally eaten with a bread. I like to serve "Royal" Lamb or Beef with a Creamy Almond Sauce (page 80) or Tandoori-style Chicken (page 90) with it.

Serves 4 to 6

2 medium potatoes

1 small head of cauliflower (you need 450 g/1 lb florets)

5 tablespoons vegetable oil

1 teaspoon cumin seeds

1 teaspoon ground cumin

1/2 teaspoon ground coriander

1/4 teaspoon ground turmeric

1/4 teaspoon cayenne pepper

1/2–1 fresh, hot green chili, very finely chopped

1/2 teaspoon ground, roasted cumin seeds (page 20)

1 teaspoon salt

Freshly ground black pepper

Boil the potatoes in their jackets and allow them to cool completely. (Day-old cooked potatoes that have been refrigerated work very well for this dish.) Peel the potatoes and cut them into 2 cm (³⁄₄ inch) dice.

Break up the cauliflower into chunky florets that are about 4 cm (1¹⁄₂ inches) across at the head and about 4 cm (1¹⁄₂ inches) long. Soak the florets in a bowl of water for 30 minutes. Drain.

Put the oil in a large, preferably nonstick, frying pan and set over medium heat. When hot, put in the cumin seeds. Let the seeds sizzle for 3–4 seconds. Now put in the cauliflower and stir it for 2 minutes. Let the cauliflower brown in spots. Cover, turn heat to low, and simmer for about 4–6 minutes or until the cauliflower is almost done but still has a hint of crispness left. Put in the diced potatoes, ground cumin, coriander, turmeric, cayenne, green chili, ground, roasted cumin seeds, salt, and some black pepper. Stir gently to mix. Continue to cook uncovered on low heat for another 3 minutes or until the potatoes are heated through.

Stir gently as you do so.

cauliflower with cumin and asafetida

Heeng zeere ki gobi

This simple, everyday dish may also be made with broccoli. Even though the broccoli will lose some of its bright green color, it will still taste very good.

Serves 4

550 g (1¼ lb) head cauliflower

3 tablespoons vegetable oil

Generous pinch of ground asafetida

½ teaspoon cumin seeds

½ medium onion, peeled and cut into very fine rings

½ –1 fresh, hot green chili, finely chopped

1 teaspoon ground cumin

½ teaspoon ground coriander

¼ teaspoon ground turmeric

⅛ –¼ teaspoon cayenne pepper, or to taste

¾ teaspoon salt, or to taste

120 ml (½ cup) water

2 teaspoons lemon juice

Break the cauliflower into florets that are about 4 cm (1½ inches) across at the head and 4–5 cm (1½ –2 inches) in length. The stem may be peeled and cut into 5 mm (¼ inch) rounds.

Put the oil in a large frying pan or wok and set over medium-high heat. When hot, put in the asafetida. A second later, put in the cumin seeds. Wait about 10 seconds and add the onion. Stir and fry for about 2 minutes or until the onion slices brown. Now put in the cauliflower and green chili. Turn heat down to medium and toss. Add the ground cumin, ground coriander, turmeric, cayenne, and salt. Toss for another minute. Add the water and lemon juice, toss, and bring to a simmer. Cover, turn heat to low, and cook for 5–7 minutes or until the cauliflower is just tender.

cauliflower with fennel and mustard seeds

Baghari phool gobi

You could serve this dish with Chicken in a Red Sweet Pepper Sauce (page 101) and rice.

Serves 6

1 large or 2 medium-sized cauliflower (you need about 900 g/2 lb florets)

7 tablespoons vegetable oil

2 teaspoons fennel seeds

1 tablespoon black mustard seeds

1 tablespoon peeled, very finely chopped garlic

$1/4$ teaspoon ground turmeric

$1/4 - 1/3$ teaspoon cayenne pepper

About $1 1/2$ teaspoons salt

About 4 tablespoons water

Cut the cauliflower into delicate florets that are no longer than 5 cm (2 inches), no wider at the head than 2.5 cm (1 inch) and about 1 cm ($1/3$ inch) thick. Put them into a bowl of water for at least 30 minutes. Drain them just before you get ready to cook.

Put the oil in a large, 25–30 cm (10–12 inch) frying pan and set over medium heat. When hot, put in the fennel and mustard seeds. As soon as the mustard seeds begin to pop, put in the finely chopped garlic. Stir and fry until the garlic pieces are lightly browned. Add the turmeric and cayenne. Stir once and quickly put in the cauliflower, salt, and water. Stir and cook on medium heat for 6–7 minutes or until the cauliflower is just done. It should retain its crispness and there should be no liquid left. If the water evaporates before the cauliflower is done, add a little more.

(If your frying pan is smaller than the suggested size, the cauliflower will take longer to cook. In that case, it might be a good idea to cover it for 5 minutes.)

carrots, peas, and potatoes flavored with cumin

Gajar, matar, aur aloo ki bhaji

Here is a simple, quick-cooking dish. Ideally, it should be made in an Indian *karhai* but if you do not have one, a large frying pan or sauté pan will do. The vegetables are cooked in a Bengali style but could easily accompany a roast chicken or grilled sausages.

Serves 6

2 large or 3 small carrots

2 small potatoes, boiled, drained and cooled

2 medium onions

1 scallion

3 tablespoons mustard oil (another vegetable oil may be substituted)

$1^{1}/_{2}$ teaspoons cumin seeds

2 dried, hot red chilies

175 g ($1^{1}/_{2}$ cups) shelled peas

About 1 teaspoon salt

$^{1}/_{4}$ teaspoon sugar

Peel the carrots and cut them first into 1 cm ($^{1}/_{2}$ inch) thick diagonal slices and then into 1 cm ($^{1}/_{2}$ inch) dice.

Peel the potatoes and cut them into 1 cm ($^{1}/_{2}$ inch) dice. Peel the onions and chop them coarsely. Cut the scallion into very, very thin slices, all the way to the end of its green section.

Put the oil in a large frying pan and set over medium heat. When hot, put in the cumin seeds. Let them sizzle for 3–4 seconds. Now put in the chilies and stir them for 3–4 seconds. Put in the chopped onions. Stir and cook for 5 minutes or until the onion pieces turn translucent. Put in the carrots and peas. Stir them for a minute. Cover, turn heat to low, and cook for about 5 minutes or until the vegetables are tender. Uncover and turn heat up slightly. Add the potatoes, salt, and sugar. Stir and cook another 2–3 minutes. Add the scallion. Stir and cook for 30 seconds.

Note: Remove the whole chilies before serving.

corn and potatoes with mustard seeds and mint

Bhutta aur aloo ki mazedar tarkari

I like to make this in the summer when fresh corn is plentiful. I take the kernels off the fresh ears but you could use frozen corn just as easily. Let the kernels defrost a bit before you cook them.

Make this dish as hot as you can manage. It tastes good that way – the sweet, hot, and sour flavors mingle to excellent effect. It can be served with almost any Indian meal. Boil the potatoes slightly ahead of time so that they have time to cool. They will be much easier to dice. The canned coconut milk gives a wonderful creaminess to the dish but you may use plain water instead if you wish.

Serves 4

3 tablespoons vegetable oil

½ teaspoon black mustard seeds

¼ teaspoon cumin seeds

1 clove garlic, peeled and finely chopped

1 medium boiling potato, boiled, peeled, and cut into 5 mm (¼ inch) dice

1 medium ripe tomato, cut into 5 mm (¼ inch) dice

4 tablespoons very finely chopped cilantro

3 tablespoons very finely chopped fresh mint

1 fresh, hot green chili, finely chopped

2 cups fresh or frozen corn kernels

85 ml (3 oz) coconut milk from a well-stirred can, or water

½ – ¾ teaspoon salt

¼ teaspoon cayenne pepper, or to taste

1 tablespoon lemon juice

Freshly ground black pepper

2 teaspoons ground, roasted cumin seeds (page 20)

Put the oil in a large, preferably nonstick, frying pan and set over medium-high heat. When hot, put in the mustard seeds and cumin seeds. As soon as the mustard seeds begin to pop – this takes just a few seconds – put in the garlic and diced potatoes. Stir and fry until the potatoes are lightly browned. Now put in the tomato, cilantro, mint, and green chili. Stir and fry for 1–2 minutes. Put in the corn and stir. Add the coconut milk or water, salt, cayenne, and lemon juice. Stir to mix and bring to a simmer. Cover, turn heat to low, and cook for 3–4 minutes or until the corn is cooked. Uncover, add some black pepper, and the ground, roasted cumin seeds. Stir to mix, and taste for the balance of seasonings.

mushrooms and potatoes cooked with garlic and ginger

Rasedar khumbi aloo

This is one of those "home-style" dishes that you rarely find in Indian restaurants. It is a thick, earthy stew that used to be made only when slim, monsoon mushrooms made a brief, seasonal appearance. Now, even in Indian cities you can buy cultivated white mushrooms all year-round. Since these mushrooms come in a variety of sizes, you will have to use your own judgment about whether you should halve them, quarter them, or leave them whole. They should end up being about the same size as the diced potatoes. You could serve this with Beef Baked with Yogurt and Black Pepper (page 69) and Gujerati Carrot Salad (page 217).

Serves 4 to 6

2 medium potatoes

350 g (12 oz) mushrooms

2.5 cm (1 inch) piece fresh ginger, peeled

6 large cloves garlic, peeled

3 tablespoons plus 250 ml (1^1/$_4$ cups) water

About 1 teaspoon salt

About ^{1}/$_3$ teaspoon ground turmeric

4 tablespoons vegetable oil

1 teaspoon cumin seeds

3 cardamom pods

3 small tomatoes, peeled (page 30) and finely chopped

1 teaspoon ground cumin

^{1}/$_2$ teaspoon ground coriander

About ^{1}/$_4$ teaspoon cayenne pepper

^{1}/$_4$ teaspoon *garam masala* (page 21)

Optional garnish: 1 tablespoon finely chopped cilantro

Boil the potatoes in their jackets. Drain and peel them. Cut them into 2.5 cm (1 inch) cubes.

Wipe the mushrooms with a damp cloth. Cut off the lower, woody part of the stems. Now, depending upon their size, halve or quarter the mushrooms, or, if they are small, leave them whole. They should be about the size of the diced potatoes.

Put the ginger and garlic into the container of a food processor or electric blender along with 3 tablespoons water. Blend until you have a fine purée.

Put the diced potatoes in a bowl. Sprinkle about ^{1}/$_4$ teaspoon of the salt and about ^{1}/$_8$ teaspoon of the turmeric over them. Toss to mix and set aside.

Put the oil in a heavy, wide, preferably nonstick, pot and set over medium heat. When hot, put in the potatoes. Stir and fry them until they are lightly browned on all sides. Remove the potato pieces with a slotted spoon and set aside on a plate. Put the cumin seeds and cardamom pods into the same pot. Stir them for 3–4 seconds. Now put in the tomatoes, the ginger-garlic paste, the ground cumin, and the ground coriander. Stir and fry until the paste becomes thick and the oil separates from it. Add ^{1}/$_4$ teaspoon turmeric and the cayenne. Stir once or twice. Put in 250 ml (1 cup) water, the potatoes, mushrooms, and ^{3}/$_4$ teaspoon salt. Stir to mix and bring to a simmer. Cover, turn heat to low, and simmer for 5 minutes. Remove the cover and turn heat up slightly. Cook, stirring gently, until you have a thick sauce. Sprinkle in the *garam masala* and stir to mix. Taste for salt.

Serve garnished with cilantro, if you wish.

Note: The cardamom pods are not meant to be eaten.

kale cooked in mustard oil

Saag

Kale is one of those highly nutritious vegetables that we eat as frequently as we can, often with just rice, a pulse, and some yogurt relish. Before you cook the kale, cut off the coarse lower stems. The weight given in this recipe is the net weight of usable leaves.

Serves 4

5 tablespoons mustard oil or extra-virgin olive oil

2–3 dried, hot red chilies

3 cloves garlic, peeled and finely chopped

1–2 fresh, hot green chilies

900 g (2 lb) kale leaves (see above), cut crosswise into 2.5 cm (1 inch) wide strips

300 ml (1¼ cups) chicken stock or water

Salt to taste (if salted stock is used, extra salt may not be needed)

Put the oil in a large pot and set over medium-high heat. When hot, put in the red chilies. Stir once or twice. The chilies will darken almost instantly. Put in the garlic. Stir until it turns golden. Put in the green chilies and stir once. Now put in the kale. Stir once or twice. Add the chicken stock or water and bring to a boil. Cover, turn heat to low, and simmer for 20–30 minutes or until the kale is tender. Remove the cover, turn heat up, and boil away all the liquid. The "sauce" should consist mainly of the oil. Taste for salt, adding as much as you need. Mix well.

sweet-and-sour okra

Kutchhi bhindi

Here is an absolutely wonderful way to cook okra. It tastes best when made with young, tender pods. It may be served with Lamb with Onions (page 64) and Mushroom *Pullao* (page 199).

Serves 4 to 6

400 g (14 oz) fresh, tender okra (*bhindi*)

7 medium-sized cloves garlic, peeled

1 dried, hot red chili
(use half if you want it very mild)

7 tablespoons water

2 teaspoons ground cumin

1 teaspoon ground coriander

½ teaspoon ground turmeric

4 tablespoons vegetable oil

1 teaspoon cumin seeds

About 1 teaspoon salt

1 teaspoon sugar

About 4 teaspoons lemon juice

Rinse off the fresh okra and pat it dry. Trim the pods by cutting off the two ends. The top end is usually trimmed with a paring knife to leave a cone-shaped head. A tiny piece of the bottom is just snipped off. Cut the okra into 2 cm (¾ inch) lengths.

Put the garlic and chili into the container of an electric blender with 3 tablespoons of the water. Blend until you have a smooth paste.

Empty the paste into a small bowl. Add the ground cumin, coriander, and turmeric. Mix.

Put the oil in a 23 cm (9 inch) frying pan or sauté pan and set over medium heat. When hot, put in the cumin seeds. As soon as the cumin seeds begin to sizzle – this happens within a few seconds – turn the heat down a bit and pour in the spice mixture. Stir and fry for about a minute. Now put in the okra, salt, sugar, lemon juice, and 4 tablespoons water. Stir to mix and bring to a gentle simmer. Cover tightly and cook on low heat for about 10 minutes or until the okra is tender. If your okra takes longer to cook, you might need to add just a little more water.

"dry" okra

Sookhi bhindi

Sometimes, when I am in the mood for some really soothing, comforting food, I make Plain Basmati Rice (page 193), *Moong Dal,* and Red Lentils with Browned Onion (page 170) and this okra. Perhaps a Tomato, Onion, and Cilantro Relish (page 215) on the side as well. The okra does not have a sauce. It is just allowed to brown slowly and gently with cumin seeds and onions. Some ground, dry spices are sprinkled over the top toward the end. It is as simple as that. And so delicious.

Serves 3 to 4

450 g (1 lb) fresh okra (*bhindi*)

8 tablespoons vegetable oil

½ teaspoon cumin seeds

1 large onion, peeled and coarsely chopped

½ teaspoon salt, or to taste

¼ teaspoon ground cumin

¼ teaspoon ground coriander

1 teaspoon ground *amchoor* or lemon juice

⅛–¼ teaspoon cayenne pepper

Wipe the okra pods with dampened paper towels. Pat dry. Cut off the conical top and the very tip of each okra pod and then cut the pods, crosswise, into 7 mm–1 cm (⅓–½ inch) segments.

Put the oil in a large, preferably nonstick, frying pan and set over medium-high heat. When hot, put in the cumin seeds. Let the seeds sizzle for 10 seconds. Put in the onion and okra, spreading the okra out evenly in the pan. Fry, stirring every now and then, for 10 minutes, spreading the okra out evenly in the pan each time you stir. The onion should begin to brown by this time. Turn heat to medium and continue to stir and fry the same way for another 5 minutes. Be gentle as you stir. Put in the salt, ground cumin, ground coriander, *amchoor* or lemon juice, and cayenne. Cook for another 5 minutes, stirring or tossing gently as you do so.

potatoes with black pepper

Bengali aloo

We take black pepper so much for granted, sprinkling tiny amounts on most foods without much thought. Apart from its taste, black pepper has a very enticing perfume and a delicate tartness as well. These properties are drawn out when the spice is used in generous quantities – as in the French *steak au poivre* or in these very Bengali potatoes. The dish is simplicity itself to make and may be eaten just as easily with European foods as with Indian. You could also stick toothpicks into the potato pieces and serve them with drinks.

Serves 4

600 g (1 lb 5 oz) potatoes (about 5 medium)

4 tablespoons vegetable oil

About ¾ teaspoon salt

1–1½ teaspoons freshly ground black pepper (a slightly coarse grind is best)

2 tablespoons very finely chopped cilantro or parsley (optional)

Boil the potatoes in their jackets and allow them to cool completely. (Day-old boiled potatoes that have been refrigerated work very well for this dish.) Peel the potatoes and cut them into 2 cm (¾ inch) dice.

Put the oil in a nonstick or very well-seasoned frying pan and set over medium heat. When hot, put in the potatoes and stir them around for a minute. Sprinkle in the salt and mix gently. Cover the potatoes and let them heat through on medium-low heat for about 5 minutes. Stir them a few times during this period. Now add the black pepper and mix gently. Cook, uncovered, for another few minutes on medium heat, stirring the potatoes every now and then and allowing them to brown slightly.

Sprinkle in the cilantro or parsley, if using. Mix and serve hot.

potatoes with sesame seeds

Til ke aloo

Here is another of those easy, delicious dishes that you might enjoy both with Indian meals and with simple dinners of roast and grilled meats.

Serves 6

900 g (2 lb) potatoes (about 8 medium)

6 tablespoons vegetable oil

2 teaspoons cumin seeds

2 teaspoons black mustard seeds

2 tablespoons sesame seeds

About 2 teaspoons salt

$1/8$–$1/2$ teaspoon cayenne pepper

1 tablespoon lemon juice

Boil the potatoes in their jackets. Drain and cool them for 3–4 hours. Peel the potatoes and dice them into 2 cm ($3/4$ inch) cubes.

Put the oil in a large, 25–30 cm (10–12 inch) frying pan and set over medium heat. (A nonstick or well-seasoned cast-iron frying pan would be ideal.) When the oil is very hot, put in the cumin seeds, mustard seeds, and sesame seeds. As soon as the seeds begin to pop – this just takes a few seconds – put in the diced potatoes. Stir and fry the potatoes for about 5 minutes.

Add the salt, cayenne, and lemon juice. Stir and fry for another 3–4 minutes.

I like the potatoes to have a few brown spots on them.

"dry" potatoes with ginger and garlic

Sookhe aloo

Can you imagine cubes of potato encrusted with a spicy, crisply browned ginger-garlic paste? Add to that a hint of fennel, if you want it. That is what these potatoes taste like. You could serve them with an Indian meal of Minced Meat with Peas (page 62), and Indian bread and a yogurt relish, or you could serve them with grilled or roast meats. It is best to make this dish in a large, nonstick frying pan or a well-used cast-iron one.

Serves 4 to 5

625 g (1 lb 6 oz) potatoes (about 5 medium)

Piece of fresh ginger, about 5 x 2.5 x 2.5 cm (2 x 1 x 1 inches), peeled and coarsely chopped

3 cloves garlic, peeled

3 tablespoons water

1/2 teaspoon ground turmeric

1 teaspoon salt

1/2 teaspoon cayenne pepper

5 tablespoons vegetable oil

1 teaspoon fennel seeds (optional)

Boil the potatoes in their jackets. Drain them and let them cool completely. Peel the potatoes and cut them into 2–2.5 cm (3/4 –1 inch) dice.

Put the ginger, garlic, 3 tablespoons water, turmeric, salt, and cayenne into the container of a food processor or blender. Blend until you have a paste. Put the oil in a large, preferably nonstick, frying pan and set over medium heat. When hot, put in the fennel seeds if you are using them. Let them sizzle for a few seconds. Now put in the ginger-garlic paste. Stir and fry for 2 minutes.

Put in the potatoes. Stir and fry over medium-high heat for 5–7 minutes or until the potatoes have a nice, golden brown crust on them.

spinach cooked with onions

Mughlai saag

I frequently serve this spinach with Chicken with Cream (page 98) and Spiced Basmati Rice (page 194).

Serves 4

900 g (2 lb) spinach, washed and trimmed

1 large onion, peeled

4 tablespoons *ghee* (page 28) or vegetable oil

¹/₂–1 fresh, hot green chili, finely chopped

1 teaspoon peeled, very finely grated fresh ginger

About 1 teaspoon salt

¹/₂ teaspoon sugar

120 ml (¹/₂ cup) water

¹/₄ teaspoon *garam masala* (page 21)

Cut the spinach, crosswise, into 1 cm (¹/₂ inch) wide strips. Chop the onion finely.

Put the *ghee* or oil in a fairly large frying pan and set over medium-high heat. When hot, put in the onions. Stir and fry for 3 minutes. Now put in the chopped spinach, green chili, ginger, salt, and sugar. Stir and cook the spinach for 5 minutes. Add the water and bring to a simmer. Cover tightly, turn heat to low, and cook for about 10 minutes. Uncover and boil away some of the extra liquid. Sprinkle *garam masala* over the top and mix.

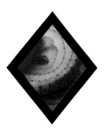

frozen spinach with potatoes

Saag aloo

In India, we combine potatoes with almost every grain, meat, and vegetable. Here is one of my favorite recipes. It may be served with Red Lamb or Beef Stew (page 70) and an Indian bread or rice.

Serves 4 to 6

300 ml (1¼ cups) plus 2 tablespoons water

550 g (1¼ lb) (2 packages) frozen leaf spinach

1 large onion, peeled

5 tablespoons vegetable oil

Pinch of ground asafetida (optional)

2 teaspoons black mustard seeds

2 cloves garlic, peeled and finely chopped

4 medium potatoes, peeled and cut roughly into 2–2.5 cm (¾–1 inch) cubes

¼ teaspoon cayenne pepper

1 teaspoon salt

Bring the 300 ml (1¼ cups) water to a boil in a pot. Put in the frozen spinach, cover and cook the spinach until it is just done. Drain in a colander and rinse under cold water.

Press out most of the liquid in the leaves (you do not have to be too thorough) and then chop them coarsely.

Cut the onions in half, lengthwise, and then crosswise into very thin slices. Put the oil in a heavy frying pan and set over medium heat. When hot, put in the asafetida, if using, and then, a second later, the mustard seeds. As soon as the mustard seeds begin to pop – this just takes a few seconds – put in the onion and garlic. Stir and fry for 2 minutes. Put in the potatoes and cayenne. Stir and fry for a minute. Now put in the spinach, salt, and 2 tablespoons water. Bring to a boil. Cover tightly, turn heat to very low, and cook gently for 40 minutes or until the potatoes are tender. Stir a few times during the cooking period and make sure that there is always a little liquid in the frying pan.

mixed vegetables in a mustard and cumin sauce

Shorvedar subzi

Indians like to cook a lot of mixed vegetable dishes and this is one of them. It may be served with any pulse and either rice or a bread. It is also a good accompaniment to almost all the meat dishes in this book.

Serves 6

450 g (1 lb) potatoes, boiled, cooled, and peeled

Vegetable oil for sautéing

1 medium-sized cauliflower, broken into fairly chunky florets

7.5 cm (3 inch) piece fresh ginger, peeled and coarsely chopped

8 cloves garlic, peeled and coarsely chopped

4 tablespoons plus $2\frac{1}{2}$ cups water

1 teaspoon black mustard seeds

1 teaspoon cumin seeds

$\frac{1}{4}$ teaspoon *kalonji*

$\frac{1}{4}$ teaspoon fennel seeds

$\frac{1}{2}$ teaspoon ground turmeric

1 teaspoon ground cumin

2 teaspoons ground coriander

1 teaspoon cayenne pepper

$1\frac{1}{4}$–$1\frac{1}{2}$ teaspoons salt

450 ml (2 cups) finely chopped tomatoes

2 medium-sized carrots, peeled and cut into 1 cm ($\frac{1}{2}$ inch) thick rounds

$\frac{1}{2}$ teaspoon *garam masala* (page 21)

150 g (1 cup) peas, fresh, or frozen and defrosted

Cut the potatoes into thick "chips" about 4 cm ($1\frac{1}{2}$ inches) long. Put the oil in a wok or frying pan and set over medium-high heat. When very hot, put in the potatoes and fry them until they are golden red. Remove with a slotted spoon to a plate lined with paper towels. Put the cauliflower into the same oil and fry until golden red. Remove with a slotted spoon and put on a plate lined with paper towels. Turn off heat and reserve the oil.

Put the ginger and garlic into the container of an electric blender or food processor along with 4 tablespoons water and blend until you have a smooth paste, pushing down with a rubber spatula when necessary.

Put 4 tablespoons of the oil used for frying into a large, preferably nonstick, frying pan and set over medium-high heat. When very hot, put in the mustard seeds and cumin seeds. As soon as the mustard seeds begin to pop – this takes just a few seconds – put in the *kalonji* and, 2 seconds later, the fennel seeds. Give one quick stir and put in the paste from the blender. Stir and fry for 2 minutes. Put in the turmeric, ground cumin, ground coriander, and cayenne. Stir once or twice and put in the salt and tomatoes. Stir and cook until most of the liquid has evaporated and the tomatoes are soft. Add 600 ml ($2\frac{1}{2}$ cups) water and bring to a simmer. Cover, turn heat to low, and simmer for about 7 minutes. Put in the carrots, cover again, and simmer for 3 minutes. Now put in the *garam masala*, peas, fried potatoes, and cauliflower. Mix gently and bring to a simmer. Cover and continue to simmer on low heat for 6–7 minutes, stirring gently now and then.

stewed tomatoes

Shorvedar timatar

It is best to make this dish in the summer, when tomatoes are plentiful. This is a "wet" dish – it has a thinnish sauce – and should be served in individual bowls. You could eat it with Beef Baked with Yogurt and Black Pepper (page 69), Spicy Baked Chicken (page 94), or Grilled Mackerel with Lemon and Cilantro (page 127). Rice should be served on the side.

Serves 4

6 medium tomatoes

3 tablespoons vegetable oil

1/2 teaspoon cumin seeds

3 cloves garlic, peeled and very finely chopped

1 large onion, peeled and chopped

1–1 1/2 fresh, hot green chilies

1 teaspoon peeled, very finely grated fresh ginger

1 teaspoon salt

1/2 –1 teaspoon sugar (preferably brown sugar)

Drop the tomatoes into a pot of rapidly boiling water for 10–15 seconds. Drain, rinse under cold water, and peel. Core the tomatoes and cut them into large chunks – roughly 2.5 cm (1 inch) cubes.

Put the oil in a medium-sized frying pan and set over medium heat. When hot, put in the cumin seeds. A few seconds later, put in the garlic. Let the garlic pieces turn a medium-brown color. Now put in the onion and green chilies. Stir and sauté for about 2 minutes. Now put in the tomatoes, ginger, salt, and sugar. Bring to a boil.

Cover, leaving the lid slightly ajar, turn heat to low, and simmer for about 10 minutes or until the tomatoes are just tender.

turnips with cilantro and mint

Rasedar shaljum

I have always had a fondness for turnips. The same, however, was not true for my three children, until I finally won them over with this dish. You could serve turnips with Lamb with Onions (page 64) and rice or an Indian bread.

Serves 6

900 g (2 lb) turnips (weight without leaves)

4 tablespoons vegetable oil

350 g (12 oz) fresh tomatoes, peeled (page 30); canned tomatoes may be substituted

2.5 cm (1 inch) cube ginger, peeled and grated to a pulp

1 tablespoon ground coriander

$^1/_2$ teaspoon ground turmeric

$^1/_4$–$^1/_2$ teaspoon cayenne pepper

425 ml (2 cups) water

3 tablespoons very finely chopped cilantro

2 tablespoons very finely chopped fresh mint

$1^1/_2$ teaspoons salt

Peel the turnips and cut them in half, lengthwise. Put the cut ends flat against your chopping board and cut them, lengthwise, into 1 cm ($^1/_3$ inch) thick slices.

Put the oil in a fairly wide frying pan and set over medium-high heat. When hot, put in the tomatoes. Stir and fry for about 2 minutes. Add the ginger, ground coriander, turmeric, and cayenne. Stir and fry another 2 minutes or until the sauce is thick and pastelike. Add the turnips, water, cilantro, mint, and salt. Cover, leaving the lid very slightly ajar, and cook on medium-low heat for 20 minutes. Stir a few times as the turnips cook. Now cover the pan tightly and cook on low heat for another 10 minutes or until the turnips are tender. You should have a little thick sauce left at the bottom of your pan that can be served spooned over the turnips.

Pulses – dried beans, split peas, and lentils – are a staple in India and help provide a large measure of the daily protein for families who eat meat rarely or are vegetarian. But pulses, by themselves, are an incomplete food and need to be complemented – at the same meal – with a grain (rice or bread) and a dairy product (such as yogurt or cheese). When nutritionists tell us today that this food combination has as much protein as a steak, I cannot help but think of the villagers in India whose basic diet, for centuries, has been *dals* (split peas) and rice or bread, washed down with a glass of buttermilk. Perhaps these villagers are not so badly off, after all!

Apart from their food value, I find pulses very versatile. Their nonassertive taste and textures allow them to be used easily in soups. They also combine beautifully with meats and vegetables to make excellent main courses.

Sometimes pulses can be hard to digest. The same Indian forebears who worked out that a nutritionally balanced vegetarian meal contained pulses, grains, and dairy products, also knew – I do not know how – that certain seasonings made pulses more digestible. Today, pulses in India are almost always cooked with at least one of the following: ginger, asafetida, and turmeric.

We have many different types of pulses in India. Some are left whole; others are split and sometimes skinned. It is the split ones that are called *dals*. The splitting helps to cook them much faster.

All pulses need to be picked over and washed, as the packages often include small stones and husks. Whole beans should either be soaked in water overnight before they are cooked or else they can be boiled in water for 2 minutes and then left to soak in the boiling water for an hour. The cooking time for all pulses varies according to their freshness. The fresher they are, the faster they cook. When cooking split peas, Indians always leave the lid slightly ajar. The reason for this is that split peas create a lot of thick froth as they cook and this blocks up the normal escape routes for the steam. So the pot boils over, creating a mess on the stove. Leaving the lid slightly ajar helps to avoid this.

All beans should be stored in tightly covered containers. On page 164, there is a description of the pulses I have used in this book.

pulses

Red split lentils Masoor dal These salmon-colored, round, split lentils are available widely in most supermarkets. They turn pale yellow during cooking and have a pleasant, mild flavor.

Whole green lentils These round, flying saucer-shaped, greenish brown lentils are very similar to our unsplit, unskinned *masoor*. They are available in all supermarkets and have the virtue of cooking quite fast.

Moong dal This is the skinned and split version of the same mung bean that is used to make bean sprouts for oriental cooking. The grains are pale yellow and somewhat elongated. This is, perhaps, the most popular North Indian *dal*. It has a mild, aristocratic flavor and is sold by Indian, Pakistani, and Greek grocers, and increasingly by many supermarkets.

Chana dal This is very similar to the yellow split peas that are sold in supermarkets, only the grains are smaller and the flavor "meatier" and sweeter. *Chana dal* is sold mainly by Indian and Pakistani grocers. Yellow split peas may be substituted for *chana dal* in my recipes.

Black-eyed beans Lobhia These excellent beans, grayish or beige ovals, graced with a dark dot, are sold widely in all supermarkets. They have a slightly smoky flavor.

Chick-peas Chhole This large, heart-shaped, beige-colored pea is sold by most supermarkets as well as South Asian and Middle Eastern grocers. It lends itself to being cooked as a spicy snack food as well as being combined with meats and vegetables.

Red kidney beans Rajma These large, dark red, kidney-shaped beans are available in all supermarkets as well as Asian grocers.

Aduki beans Ma These smaller red beans look like the children of red kidney beans. For some reason, they are sold by their Japanese name, *aduki*.

red split lentils with cumin seeds

Masoor dal

This salmon-colored split pea turns dull yellow when cooked. It is sold as "Egyptian lentils" in some Middle Eastern stores. It is best served with a rice dish and almost any Indian meat and vegetable you like.

Serves 4 to 6

200 g (1 cup) red split lentils (*masoor dal*), picked over, washed, and drained

1 liter (4$^1/_3$ cups) water

2 thin slices unpeeled ginger

$^1/_2$ teaspoon ground turmeric

1 teaspoon salt, or to taste

3 tablespoons *ghee* (page 28) or vegetable oil

Pinch of ground asafetida (optional)

1 teaspoon cumin seeds

1 teaspoon ground coriander

$^1/_4$ teaspoon cayenne pepper

2 tablespoons finely chopped cilantro

Combine the lentils and water in a heavy pot. Bring to a simmer. Remove any scum that collects at the top. Add the ginger and turmeric. Stir to mix. Cover, leaving the lid very slightly ajar, turn heat to low, and simmer gently for 1$^1/_2$ hours or until the lentils are tender. Stir every 5 minutes during the last 30 minutes to prevent sticking. Add the salt and stir to mix. Remove ginger slices.

Put the *ghee* or oil in a small frying pan and set over medium heat. When hot, put in the asafetida, if using. A second later, put in the cumin seeds. Let the seeds sizzle for a few seconds. Now put in the ground coriander and cayenne. Stir once and then quickly pour the contents of the frying pan – the *ghee* and spices – into the pot with the lentils. Stir to mix.

Sprinkle the cilantro over the top when you serve.

red split lentils with cabbage

Masoor dal aur band gobi

I eat this with rice and Lemony Chicken with Cilantro (page 95).

Serves 4 to 6

200 g (1¼ cups) red split lentils (*masoor dal*), picked over, washed, and drained

1.2 liters (5 cups) water

½ teaspoon ground turmeric

5 tablespoons vegetable oil

1 teaspoon cumin seeds

2–4 cloves garlic, peeled and finely chopped

1 medium onion, peeled and cut into fine slices

225 g (½ lb) cored and finely shredded cabbage

1–2 fresh, hot green chilies, finely sliced

1½ teaspoons salt

1 medium tomato, peeled (page 30) and finely chopped

½ teaspoon peeled, finely grated fresh ginger

Put the lentils and water into a heavy pot and bring to a boil. Remove any scum that collects at the top. Add the turmeric and stir to mix. Cover, leaving the lid very slightly ajar, turn heat down to low, and simmer gently for 1¼ hours. Stir a few times during the last 30 minutes.

While the lentils cook, heat the oil in a 20–23 cm (8–9 inch) frying pan over medium heat. When hot, put in the cumin seeds. Let them sizzle for 3–4 seconds. Now put in the garlic. As soon as the garlic pieces begin to brown, put in the onion, cabbage, and green chilies. Stir and fry the cabbage mixture for about 10 minutes or until it begins to brown and turn slightly crisp. Stir in ¼ teaspoon of the salt. Turn off the heat under the frying pan.

When the lentils have cooked for 1¼ hours, add the remaining 1¼ teaspoon salt, the tomato, and ginger to the pot. Stir to mix. Cover and cook another 10 minutes. Add the cabbage mixture and any remaining oil in the frying pan. Stir to mix and bring to a simmer.

Simmer, uncovered, for 2–3 minutes or until the cabbage is heated through.

small yellow split peas

Chana dal

Of all the *dals*, this one perhaps has the "meatiest" taste. If you cannot find it, substitute yellow split peas. You could serve this *dal* with rice and Chicken with Tomatoes and *Garam Masala* (page 99).

Serves 4 to 6

225 g (1½ cups) *chana dal* or yellow split peas, picked over, washed, and drained

1.2 liters (5 cups) water

½ teaspoon ground turmeric

2 thin slices unpeeled ginger

¾–1 teaspoon salt

¼ teaspoon *garam masala* (page 21)

3 tablespoons *ghee* (page 28) or vegetable oil

½ teaspoon cumin seeds

1–2 cloves garlic, peeled and chopped

¼–½ teaspoon red chilli powder

Put the *dal* in a heavy pot along with the water. Bring to a boil and remove any surface scum. Add the turmeric and ginger. Cover, leaving the lid very slightly ajar, turn heat to low, and simmer gently for 1½ hours or until the *dal* is tender. Stir every 5 minutes or so during the last 30 minutes to prevent sticking. Add the salt and *garam masala*. Stir to mix. Remove ginger slices.

Put the *ghee* or oil in a small frying pan and set over medium heat. When hot, put in the cumin seeds. A couple of seconds later, put in the garlic. Stir and fry until the garlic pieces are lightly browned. Put the chili powder into the pan. Immediately, lift the pan off the heat and pour its entire contents – *ghee* and spices – into the pot with the *dal*. Stir to mix.

whole green lentils with garlic and onion

You could serve this simple but tasty dish with Goan-style Hot and Sour Pork (page 82), Simple Buttery Rice with Onion (page 194), and Gujerati-style Green Beans (page 131).

Serves 4 to 6

4 tablespoons vegetable oil

½ teaspoon cumin seeds

4 cloves garlic, peeled and finely chopped

1 medium onion, peeled and chopped

200 g (1 cup) whole green lentils, picked over, washed, and drained

720 ml (3 cups) water

1 teaspoon salt

⅛–¼ teaspoon cayenne pepper

Put the oil in a heavy pot and set over medium heat. When hot, put in the cumin seeds. A few seconds later, put in the garlic. Stir and fry until the garlic pieces turn a medium-brown color. Now put in the onions. Stir and fry until the onion pieces begin to turn brown at the edges. Put in the lentils and the water. Bring to a boil. Cover, turn heat to low, and simmer for about an hour or until the lentils are tender. Add the salt and the cayenne. Stir to mix and simmer gently for another 5 minutes.

whole green lentils with spinach and ginger

This very nourishing dish goes well with Beef Baked with Yogurt and Black Pepper (page 69) and Lamb with Onions (page 64).

Serves 6

200 g (1 cup) whole green lentils, picked over, washed, and drained

720 ml (3 cups) water

6 tablespoons vegetable oil

1–2 fresh, hot green chilies, finely sliced

1 teaspoon peeled, very finely grated fresh ginger

8 well-packed tablespoons chopped cilantro

550 g (1¼ lb) fresh spinach, trimmed, washed, and chopped

2 teaspoons salt

Freshly ground black pepper

2 tablespoons lemon juice, or more, according to taste

Put the lentils and water into a heavy pot and bring to a boil. Cover, turn heat to low, and simmer for 1 hour.

Put the oil in a pot large enough to hold the spinach and set over medium heat. When hot, put in the green chilies and the ginger. Stir and fry for 10 seconds. Add the cilantro and spinach. Stir and cook until the spinach has wilted. Now put in the cooked lentils and the salt. Stir to mix and bring to a simmer. Cover and cook very gently for 25 minutes. Add the black pepper and lemon juice, stir to mix, and cook uncovered for 5 minutes. Check seasonings.

red kidney beans

Punjabi rajma

Rajma, red kidney beans, are cooked slowly in Punjabi villages, often in the ashes of a *tandoor* or clay oven. I used to cook them for 4½ hours on top of the stove but have now found a much quicker method. This dish may also be made with aduki beans or an equal mixture of red kidney beans and aduki beans. These beans may be served with Red Lamb or Beef Stew (page 70) and an Indian bread.

Serves 4 to 6

175 g (1¼ cups) red kidney beans, picked over, washed, and drained

1.5 liters (6 cups) water

3 thin slices of unpeeled ginger plus ½ teaspoon peeled, very finely chopped ginger

About 1 teaspoon salt

1½ tablespoons lemon juice

¼ teaspoon *garam masala* (page 21)

150 ml (⅔ cup) heavy cream

3 tablespoons *ghee* (page 28) or vegetable oil

½ teaspoon cumin seeds

1 clove garlic, peeled and finely chopped

2 dried, hot red chilies

Put the beans and water into a heavy pot and bring to a boil. Turn heat to low and simmer for 2 minutes. Turn off the heat and let the beans sit, uncovered, for 1 hour. Add the 3 slices of ginger to the beans and bring them to a boil again. Fast boil for 10 minutes, then cover, leaving the lid very slightly ajar. Turn heat to low and simmer gently for 1 hour. Discard the ginger slices.

You may now mash the beans against the sides of the pot or take half the beans and their liquid and purée them in a blender. Pour this puréed paste back into the pot of beans. This gives the dish a pleasant texture. Add the salt, lemon juice, *garam masala,* and cream. Stir to mix and check seasonings.

Put the *ghee* or oil in a small frying pan and set over medium heat. When hot, put in the cumin seeds. Two seconds later, put in the finely chopped garlic and the ½ teaspoon chopped ginger. Stir and fry until the garlic browns lightly. Put in the red chilies. Stir them once and then pour the contents of the frying pan – the *ghee* and seasonings – into the pot with the beans. Stir to mix.

Note: The whole red chilies are not meant to be eaten.

moong dal and red lentils with browned onion

Mili moong aur masoor dal

Here two pulses are combined in an earthy, wholesome, and utterly delicious preparation, one that I eat at least once or twice a week. I like to serve it with Plain Basmati Rice (page 193) and any meat or vegetable dish.

Serves 6 to 8

175 g (1 cup) *moong dal*

175 g (1 cup) red split lentils (*masoor dal*)

1.2 liters (5 cups) water

$1/2$ teaspoon ground turmeric

$1^1/4$ –$1^1/2$ teaspoons salt

4 tablespoons vegetable oil or *ghee* (page 28)

Generous pinch of ground asafetida

1 teaspoon cumin seeds

3–5 dried, hot red chilies

1 small onion, peeled and cut into very thin half-rings

Pick over the *moong dal* and red lentils. Combine them in a bowl and wash in several changes of water. Drain. Put in a heavy pot. Add the water and turmeric. Stir and bring to a simmer. (Do not let it boil over.) Cover in such a way as to leave the lid just very slightly ajar, turn heat to low, and simmer gently for 40–50 minutes or until the pulses are tender. Stir a few times during the cooking. Add the salt and mix. Leave covered, on very low heat, as you do the next step.

Put the oil or *ghee* in a small frying pan and set over high heat. When hot, put in the asafetida, then, a second later, the cumin seeds. Let the cumin seeds sizzle for a few seconds. Put in the red chilies. As soon as they turn dark red (this takes just a few seconds), put in the onion. Stir and fry on medium-high heat until the onion turns quite brown and crisp. You may need to turn the heat down a bit toward the end to prevent burning. Now lift up the lid of the *dal* pot and pour in the contents of the frying pan, oil as well as spices and onion.

Cover the pot immediately to trap the aromas.

"dry" moong dal

Sookhi moong dal

Not all *dals* are cooked to be thin and soupy. Here the grains stand out, all plump and separate, and the *dal* has a fairly dry look. It is usually not eaten with rice but with breads and other meats and vegetables. I love to sprinkle some crisp, browned onions over the top, just before I serve it. You will find a recipe for the onions on page 221.

Serves 4 to 6

200 g (1 cup) *moong dal*

900 ml (4 cups) plus 1 tablespoon plus 225 ml (1 cup) water

1 teaspoon ground coriander

1 teaspoon ground cumin

¼ teaspoon ground turmeric

⅛ –¼ teaspoon cayenne pepper

2 tablespoons vegetable oil

About ½ teaspoon salt

2 tablespoons *ghee* (page 28)

½ teaspoon cumin seeds

1 dried, hot red chili (optional)

Pick over the *dal* and wash it in several changes of water. Drain. Put the *dal* in a bowl. Pour about 900 ml (4 cups) water over it and let it soak for 3 hours. Drain.

Combine the coriander, ground cumin, turmeric, cayenne, and 1 tablespoon water in a small cup.

Put the oil in a heavy pot and set over medium heat. When hot, put in the spice mixture from the cup and stir once. Quickly put in the drained *dal*. Stir to mix. Add the salt and 225 ml (1 cup) water. Bring to a boil. Cover tightly, turn heat to very low, and cook for 15 minutes. The *dal* grains should now be quite tender.

Just before you sit down to eat, put the hot *dal* into a serving bowl. Heat the *ghee* in a small pot or a small frying pan. When it is very hot, put in the cumin seeds. Let them sizzle for a few seconds. Now put in the red chili, if using, and stir it about for 2–3 seconds – it should puff up and darken. Now pour the *ghee* and spices over the cooked *dal*. You may stir to mix or else leave the spices on the top as a kind of garnish.

If you decide to use the fried onions, you may sprinkle these over the *dal* at the last minute as well.

Note: Those unfamiliar with Indian foods should be warned that the whole chili is very hot and not meant to be eaten – except by those who know what they are doing.

sour chick-peas

Khatte chhole

Known variously as chick-peas, garbanzos, and, in India, *chholas* and *kabuli chanas*, this unsplit, heart-shaped pulse provides North Indians with some of their tastiest snack foods. As a child in Delhi, I much preferred buying my *chholas* from street vendors. They were invariably more sour, spicier, and tastier than anything produced at home. In this recipe, I have tried to reproduce that elusive taste that made me an addict of the dish many years ago.

I serve *khatte chhole* with vegetables, meats, and rice.

Serves 6

350 g (2¼ cups) chick-peas picked over, washed, and drained

1.75 liters (7½ cups) water

3 medium onions, peeled and very finely chopped

About 2½ teaspoons salt

1 fresh, hot green chili, finely chopped

1 tablespoon peeled, very finely grated fresh ginger

4 tablespoons lemon juice

6 tablespoons vegetable oil

2 medium tomatoes, finely chopped

1 tablespoon ground coriander

1 tablespoon ground cumin

½ teaspoon ground turmeric

2 teaspoons *garam masala* (page 21)

½ teaspoon cayenne pepper

Soak the chick-peas in the water for 20 hours. Put the chick-peas and their soaking liquid into a large pot and bring to a boil. Cover, lower heat, and simmer gently for 1½ hours or until the chick-peas are tender. Strain the chick-peas and save the cooking liquid.

Put 2 tablespoons of the chopped onions, ½ teaspoon of the salt and the green chili, ginger, and lemon juice into a small cup. Mix well and set aside.

Put the oil in a heavy, wide, pot and set over medium-high heat. When hot, put in the remaining chopped onions. Stir and fry for 8–10 minutes or until the onion bits develop reddish brown spots. Add the tomatoes. Continue to stir and fry for another 5–6 minutes, mashing the tomato pieces with the back of a slotted spoon. Put in the coriander, cumin, and turmeric. Stir and cook for about 30 seconds. Now put in the drained chick-peas, 400 ml (1¾ cups) of their cooking liquid, the remaining 2 teaspoons salt, the *garam masala*, and cayenne. Stir to mix and bring to a simmer. Cover, turn heat to low, and cook very gently for 20 minutes. Stir a few times during this period. Add the mixture in the cup. Stir again to mix. Serve hot or lukewarm.

black-eyed beans with mushrooms

Lohbia aur khumbi

I like this bean dish so much I often find myself eating it up with a spoon, all by itself. At a meal, I serve it with Red Lamb or Beef Stew (page 70) or with Chicken in a Fried Onion Sauce (page 93). Rice or Indian breads should be served on the side.

Serves 6

225 g (1³/₄ cups) dried black-eyed beans, picked over, washed, and drained

1.2 liters (5 cups) water

225 g (¹/₂ lb) fresh mushrooms

6 tablespoons vegetable oil

1 teaspoon cumin seeds

2.5 cm (1 inch) cinnamon stick

1¹/₂ medium onions, peeled and chopped

4 cloves garlic, peeled and very finely chopped

4 medium tomatoes, peeled (page 30) and chopped

2 teaspoons ground coriander

1 teaspoon ground cumin

¹/₂ teaspoon ground turmeric

¹/₄ teaspoon cayenne pepper

2 teaspoons salt

Freshly ground black pepper

3 tablespoons chopped cilantro (fresh parsley may be substituted)

Put the beans and water into a heavy pot and bring to a boil. Cover, turn heat to low and simmer gently for 2 minutes. Turn off the heat and let the pot sit, covered and undisturbed, for 1 hour.

While the pot is resting, cut the mushrooms through their stems into 3 mm (¹/₈ inch) thick slices.

Put the oil in a frying pan and set over medium-high heat. When hot, put in the cumin seeds and the cinnamon stick. Let them sizzle for 5–6 seconds. Now put in the onions and garlic. Stir and fry until the onion pieces turn brown at the edges. Put in the mushrooms. Stir and fry until the mushrooms wilt. Now put in the tomatoes, ground coriander, cumin, turmeric, and cayenne. Stir and cook for a minute. Cover, turn heat to low, and let this mixture cook in its own juices for 10 minutes. Turn off the heat under the frying pan.

Bring the beans to a boil again. Cover, turn heat to low, and simmer for 20–30 minutes or until the beans are tender. To this bean and water mixture, add the mushroom mixture, salt, black pepper, and cilantro or parsley. Stir to mix and bring to a simmer. Simmer, uncovered, on medium-low heat for another 30 minutes. Stir occasionally. Remove the cinnamon stick before serving.

Bread and rice are the staple accompaniments eaten with every single Indian meal. I have included in this chapter detailed cooking instructions for the four best-known types of Indian bread – layered bread (*parathas*), flat bread (*chapatis*), deep-fried puffy bread (*pooris*), and leavened oven bread (*naan*) – all wonderful breads to impress your family and guests.

And if you want to serve rice too, it can be prepared in so many different ways, from simple Spiced Basmati Rice, which beautifully complements many of the savory dishes in this book, to the delicious Mushroom *Pullao*, a vegetarian meal in itself!

accompaniments

breads

There are all kinds of breads in India, most of them unleavened, eaten in the North at every single meal. Many of these everyday breads are made with a *very* finely ground wholemeal flour that we call *ata*. I find that the flour that approximates *ata* best is a wheatmeal flour because it has just enough bran in it to give it body without making it too coarse for our soft, pliable breads. Of course, if you have access to Indian grocers and can buy *ata* (sometimes called *chapati* flour) do, by all means, use it.

Some of our breads, such as the *poori*, are deep-fried. The ideal utensil for this is the Indian *karhai* because it is very economical on oil and because it prevents hot oil from splashing onto the stove. A deep frying pan may be used as a substitute.

Many other breads are cooked on a *tava*, a concave cast-iron plate that is heated before breads such as *chapatis* and *parathas* are slapped onto it. As I have suggested in the chapter on equipment, a cast-iron frying pan makes a perfectly adequate substitute.

You will find one other kind of bread in this chapter. It is really a savory pancake and is made, not with flour but with a split pea (*moong dal*) batter. Such pancakes are a very common breakfast and snack food in India, especially in the West and South.

layered bread

Paratha

We eat these triangular breads frequently with our meals, with vegetables such as Spicy Green Beans (page 132) or Eggplant Cooked in the Pickling Style (page 136) and meats such as Chicken with Cream (page 98).

Makes 12 parathas

175 g (1³/₄ cups) sifted wheatmeal flour

185 g (1³/₄ cups) plain flour plus some extra for dusting

¹/₂ teaspoon salt

About 10 tablespoons vegetable oil, or melted *ghee* (page 28)

237 ml (1 cup) water

Put the 2 flours and salt in a bowl. Dribble 2 tablespoons of the oil or melted *ghee* over the top. Rub the oil in with your fingertips until the mixture resembles coarse breadcrumbs. Slowly add the water and gather the flour together to form a softish ball.

Empty the ball onto a clean work surface. Knead for about 10 minutes or until you have a smooth, soft, but not sticky, dough. Form a ball. Rub the ball with about ¹/₄ teaspoon of the oil and slip it into a plastic bag for 30 minutes or longer.

Set a large, cast-iron frying pan over medium-low heat. Meanwhile, knead the dough again and form 12 equal balls. Keep 11 of them covered while you work with the twelfth. Flatten this ball and dust it with some plain flour. Roll it out into a 15 cm (6 inch) round, dusting your work surface with flour whenever necessary. Spread ¹/₄ teaspoon of the oil over the surface of the *paratha* and fold it in half. Spread about ¹/₈ teaspoon of the oil over the surface of the half that is on top and fold it into half again to form a triangle. Roll out this triangle into a larger triangle with 18 cm (7 inch) sides. Dust with flour whenever necessary.

Brush the hot frying pan with ¹/₄ teaspoon of the oil and slap the *paratha* onto it. Let the *paratha* cook for a minute. Now brush the top generously with 1 teaspoon oil. The brushing will take about 30 seconds. Turn the *paratha* over and cook the second side for a minute or so. Both sides should have reddish gold spots. Move the *paratha* around so all ends are exposed evenly to the heat. Put the cooked *paratha* on a plate. Cover either with an inverted plate or with a piece of aluminum foil. Make all the *parathas* this way.

If *parathas* are not to be eaten right away, wrap them tightly in foil. The whole bundle of *parathas* may then be heated in a 200°C/400°F oven for 15–20 minutes.

flat bread
Chapati

Sometimes small and delicate and at other times large and thick, this is the basic, flat and disklike Indian bread eaten over most of North India. It is made out of a very finely ground wholemeal flour that is sold in Indian shops as *ata* or "*chapati* flour." I find that finely sifted wheatmeal flour makes an adequate substitute. If you are using the wheatmeal flour, make sure you sift it before you weigh it. Some people like to add a little bit of salt to the flour. This should be done before you make the dough.

Chapati dough has to be quite soft. The amount of water you use to form it will vary with the type of flour and the general humidity in the air. Use the quantity of water I have suggested as a guideline but don't be afraid to use more or less as you see fit. Because the dough is soft, *chapatis* are rolled out into their round, disk shape with the assistance of a fair amount of extra flour.

Chapatis are traditionally cooked on a *tava*, a slightly concave, circular, cast-iron plate, which is left to heat by itself before the first *chapati* is slapped onto it. This preheating prevents the *chapati* from becoming hard and brittle. If you don't have a *tava*, you could use a heavy, cast-iron frying pan.

First, the *chapati* is cooked briefly on both sides. Then, in India at any rate, it is put directly on top of live charcoal. It is this exposure to intense heat that makes it puff up. Since few of us have live charcoal in our kitchens anymore, this same puffing-up process may be done, if you have a gas stove, by putting the *chapati* directly on top of a low gas flame. The time a *chapati* spends sitting on the flame is very brief and, for some reason, it does not burn or catch fire.

You could, if you like, spread a little butter or *ghee* on top of the *chapati* as soon as it is made. Usually, *chapatis* are stacked, one on top of the other, as they are being made, and kept covered with a napkin, so they stay hot. Needless to say, they deflate in the process but still taste wonderful. The only way to eat a puffed-up *chapati* is to eat it as it comes off the stove.

Perfection in *chapati*-making does come with practice. If your first few *chapatis* turn out a little odd-shaped, remember that they will still taste good.

Chapatis freeze well and defrost easily, without losing taste or texture.

Makes about 15 chapatis

250 g (1³/₄ cups) sifted wheatmeal flour
plus extra for dusting
About 175 ml (³/₄ cup) water

Put the 250 g (1³/₄ cups) flour in a bowl. Slowly add the water, gathering the flour together as you do so to form a soft dough. Knead the dough for 6–8 minutes or until it is smooth. Put the dough in a bowl. Cover with a damp cloth and leave for 30 minutes.

Set an Indian *tava* or a cast-iron frying pan over medium-low heat for 10 minutes. When it is very hot, turn the heat to low.

Knead the dough again and divide it, roughly, into 15 parts. It will be fairly sticky, so rub your hands with a little flour when handling it.

Take one part of the dough and form a ball. Flour your work surface generously and roll the ball in it. Press down on the ball to make a patty. Now roll this patty out, dusting it very frequently with flour, until it is about 14 cm (5½ inches) in diameter. Pick up this *chapati* and pat it between your hands to shake off extra flour and then slap it onto the hot *tava* or frying pan. Let it cook on low heat for about a minute. Its underside should develop white spots. Turn the *chapati* over (I use my hands to do this but you could use a pair of tongs) and cook for about 30 seconds on the second side. Take the pan off the stove and put the *chapati* directly on top of the low flame. It should puff up in seconds.

Turn the *chapati* over and let the second side sit on the flame for a few seconds. Put the *chapati* on a deep plate lined with a large napkin. Fold the napkin over the *chapati*. Make all the *chapatis* this way.

Ideally, *chapatis* should be eaten as soon as they are made. But if you wish to eat them later, wrap the whole stack in aluminum foil and either refrigerate for a day or freeze. The *chapatis* may be reheated, still wrapped in foil, in a 220°C/425°F oven for 15–20 minutes.

deep-fried, puffy bread
Poori

Pooris look like puffed-up balloons. They are crispy-soft, delicious, and may be eaten with almost all Indian meats, vegetables, and pulses. They are also easy to make. Rolled out disks of dough are put into hot oil – the oil *must* be hot or the *pooris* will not "blister" and puff – and cook magically in a few seconds. As *pooris* are best eaten hot, I have taught my entire family how to make them. I make three *pooris* per person. Then, if anyone wants more, they can go into the kitchen and make their own (Note: You should always supervise children in the kitchen.) When my children were young, our *poori* dinners invariably turned into a "happening" with flour-covered children and husband wandering in and out of the kitchen, rolling pin in hand and a look of great achievement on their faces.

A word of caution: As cooking oil for *pooris* is hot, care should be taken not to splash it around. An Indian *karhai* is the safest and most economical utensil for deep-frying. If you do not have one, use a *deep* frying pan. Do not drop the *poori* into the oil from a great height or it will splash. Bring your hand as close to the surface of the oil as you can and lay the *poori* over it. Oil has no steam and will not burn you unless you touch it. When turning the *poori* over, bring it first to the edge of your utensil and then use the edge to help you turn it over. This, again, is to avoid splashes. Drain the cooked *poori* over the oil for a second or two before putting it on a plate. If you take these simple precautions (necessary for any deep-frying), *poori*-making can be fun.

Makes 12 pooris

110 g (1 cup) sifted wheatmeal flour

110 g (1 cup) plain flour

½ teaspoon salt

2 tablespoons vegetable oil plus
more for deep-frying

100 ml (½ cup) water

Put the 2 flours and salt in a bowl. Dribble 2 tablespoons oil over the top. Rub the oil in with your fingers so the mixture resembles coarse breadcrumbs. Slowly add the water to form a stiff ball of dough. Empty the ball onto a clean work surface. Knead it for 10–12 minutes or until it is smooth. Form a ball. Rub about ¼ teaspoon oil on the ball and slip it into a plastic bag. Set it aside for 30 minutes.

Knead the dough again, and divide it into 12 equal balls. Keep 11 of them covered while you work with the twelfth. Flatten this ball and roll it out into a 13–14 cm (5–5½ inch) round. If you have the space, roll out all the *pooris* and keep them in a single layer, covered with plastic wrap.

Put about 2.5 cm (1 inch) of oil in a small, deep frying pan and set over medium heat. Let it get very hot. Meanwhile, line a plate with paper towels. Lift up one *poori* and lay it carefully over the surface of the hot oil. It might sink to the bottom but it should rise in seconds and begin to sizzle. Using the back of a slotted spoon, push the *poori* gently into the oil with tiny, swift strokes. Within seconds, the *poori* will puff up. Turn it over and cook the second side for about 10 seconds. Remove it with a slotted spoon and put it on the plate. Make all the *pooris* this way. The first layer on the plate may be covered with a layer of paper towels. More *pooris* can then be spread over the top.

Serve the *pooris* hot.

leavened oven bread

Naan

Naans and other similar flat leavened breads are eaten all the way from the Caucasus down through northwestern India. In India, the baking is done in very hot clay ovens or *tandoors*. The breads are slapped onto the inside walls and cook quite happily alongside skewered chickens. At home, where most of us do not have *tandoors*, *naans* can be baked by using both the oven and the grill.

Naans may be cooked both with and without egg. If you decide not to use the egg, just increase the yogurt by about 4 tablespoons.

Naans may be eaten with almost any Indian meat or vegetable.

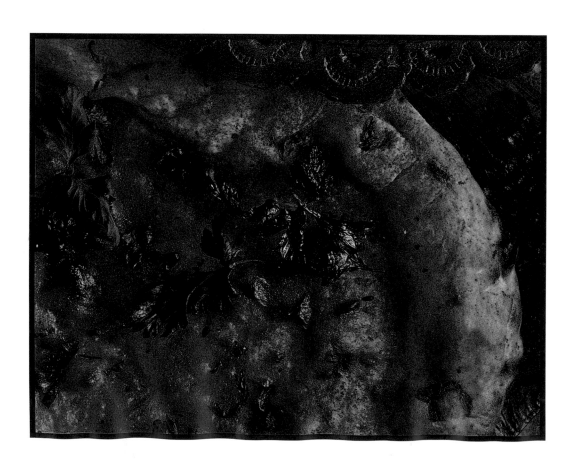

Makes 6 large breads

150 ml (²/₃ cup) hot milk

2 teaspoons granulated sugar

2 teaspoons dried active yeast

450 g (3³/₄ cups) plain flour

¹/₂ teaspoon salt

1 teaspoon baking powder

2 tablespoons vegetable oil plus
a little extra

150 ml (²/₃ cup) plain yogurt,
lightly beaten

1 large egg, lightly beaten

Put the milk in a bowl. Add 1 teaspoon of the sugar, and the yeast. Stir to mix. Set aside for 15–20 minutes or until the yeast has dissolved and the mixture is frothy.

Sift the flour, salt, and baking powder into a large bowl. Add the remaining 1 teaspoon sugar, the yeast mixture, 2 tablespoons vegetable oil, and the yogurt and egg. Mix and form a ball of dough.

Empty the ball of dough onto a clean work surface and knead it for 10 minutes or more, until it is smooth and satiny. Form into a ball. Pour about ¹/₄ teaspoon oil into a large bowl and roll the ball of dough in it. Cover the bowl with a piece of plastic wrap and set aside in a warm, draft-free place for 1 hour or until the dough has doubled in bulk.

Preheat your oven to the highest temperature. Put the heaviest baking pan you own to heat in the oven. Preheat your broiler.

Punch down the dough and knead it again. Divide it into 6 equal balls. Keep 5 of them covered while you work with the sixth. Roll this ball into a tear-shaped *naan*, about 25 cm (10 inches) in length and about 13 cm (5 inches) at its widest. Remove the hot baking pan from the oven and slap the *naan* onto it. Put it immediately into the oven for 3 minutes. It should puff up. Now place the baking pan and *naan* under the broiler, about 7.5–10 cm (3–4 inches) away from the heat, for about 30 seconds or until the top of the *naan* browns slightly. Wrap the *naan* in a clean dish towel. Make all the *naans* this way and serve hot.

moong dal pancakes with peas

Gujerati poore

Savory pancakes made out of split peas, or rice and split peas, provide much of India with a nourishing snack food. These protein-rich pancakes are also eaten by many vegetarian Indians at breakfast, usually accompanied by a chutney and a glass of fresh buttermilk. You could also serve them with tea.

Makes about 9 pancakes

185 g (1 cup) *moong dal*, picked over, washed, and drained

1 liter (4$^1/_3$ cups) plus 85 ml ($^1/_3$ cup) plus 1 tablespoon water

50 g ($^1/_2$ cup) shelled peas

2.5 cm (1 inch) cube ginger, peeled and coarsely chopped

2–3 cloves garlic, peeled

1–2 fresh, hot green chilies, cut into 4 pieces each

1 teaspoon salt

$^1/_4$ teaspoon ground turmeric

$^1/_2$ medium onion, peeled and minced

2 tablespoons finely chopped cilantro

$^1/_4$ teaspoon baking soda

About 120 ml ($^1/_2$ cup) vegetable oil

Put the *dal* in a bowl. Add 1 liter (1¾ pints) water and soak for 5 hours. Drain.

Drop the peas into boiling water for 3–4 minutes or until they are tender. Drain and chop coarsely.

Combine the ginger, garlic, green chilies, salt, turmeric, *dal*, and 85 ml ($^1/_3$ cup) plus 1 tablespoon water in the container of an electric blender. Blend until you have a smooth batter. Let the machine run for 2–3 minutes more so the batter gets light and airy.

Empty the batter into a bowl. Add the onion and cilantro and peas. Mix. The batter may now be covered and refrigerated, if you like, for up to 24 hours. Just before you get ready to cook, add the baking soda and mix it in. Remember to stir the batter before you make each pancake.

Brush a 20 cm (8 inch) nonstick frying pan with about 1 teaspoon of the oil and set it over medium-low heat. Remove about 55 ml ($^1/_4$ cup) of batter. When the oil is hot, drop this batter right in the center of the pan. Now, place the rounded bottom of a soupspoon on the center of the blob of batter. Using a gentle but continuous spiral motion, spread the batter outward with the back of the spoon, smoothing out any ridges along the way. Make a pancake that is about 14–15 cm (5½–6 inches) in diameter. Dribble a teaspoon of oil over the pancake and another ½ teaspoon around its edges. Cover the pan and let the pancake cook for 2 minutes or until its underside turns a reddish color. Uncover the pan and turn the pancake over. Cook the pancake on the reverse side for 1½ minutes or until it develops small red spots. Remove the pancake and put it on a plate. Cover with a second plate, inverted over the first. Make all the pancakes this way, making sure you stir the batter each time.

These pancakes are best eaten hot, just as soon as they are made. You could, if you wish, stack them on a sheet of aluminum foil and then wrap them up. The whole thing can be heated in an oven at 220°C/425°F for 15 minutes.

rice

My Western friends are always telling me that they cannot cook rice. They can hardly be blamed for their phobia. It starts, I think, with inadequate – inaccurate, in fact – instructions on rice boxes that invariably suggest using far more water than rice really requires. The rice ends up being mushy and the people who are cooking it often think that it is their fault. It is not.

There are, actually, many methods of cooking rice well. You will find several in the chapter that follows. Rice can be cooked like pasta, in a lot of boiling water until it is half done. Then it can be drained and "dried off" in a slow oven. Rice can be cooked completely on top of the stove with just the correct amount of water needed for absorption. Or you can start cooking rice on top of the stove with just the amount of water needed for absorption and then finish it off in the oven. The method you choose depends upon the recipe and what you want the rice to do.

If you are unsure about cooking rice, just follow my recipes carefully and you should not go wrong.

There are a few things that are worth remembering when cooking rice.

1 Use a heavy pot with a very tight-fitting lid. If you have a tin-lined copper pot hanging decoratively in your kitchen, this is your chance to use it. An enameled, cast-iron pot is also good for rice. I find that such pots generally have fairly loose-fitting lids. There is a very quick remedy for this. Just cover the pot tightly with a sheet of aluminum foil first and then with its own lid. You can also make good rice in heavy, stainless steel pots. Anytime you are unsure about the fitting of the lid, interpose a layer of aluminum foil between it and the pot. Be sure to crinkle the edges of the foil so that hardly any steam escapes. In many of my recipes, the rice ends up by cooking in steam. If too much of it escapes, the rice will not cook properly.

2 For best results, rice should be washed in several changes of water and then soaked for about 30 minutes before it is cooked. The washing gets rid of the starchy powder left over from the milling process. The soaking lets each grain absorb water so it sticks less to the next grain while it is cooking.

3 If you are cooking rice with just enough water or stock needed for absorption, what is the correct proportion of liquid to rice? I like to measure my rice in a clear measuring cup and I never use more than 1½ parts liquid to 1 part rice. If I have soaked the rice, my ratio changes to 1⅓ parts liquid to 1 part rice.

4 Sometimes I sauté my rice before I add liquid to it. This also helps to keep the grains separate. When you sauté rice, do it gently. Some types of rice grains, such as basmati, are very delicate, particularly after they have been soaked. If you sauté too vigorously, the grains break up into small pieces.

5 Once I have covered my rice pot with a lid, I like to cook it on very, very low heat. If you cannot adjust your heat very, very low, use an ovenproof pot to begin with, cover it tightly as instructed, and pop it into a preheated 170°C/325°F/Gas 3 oven for 25 minutes.

6 Resist any urge you may have to peep into a covered pot of rice before the cooking time is over. Precious steam will escape and the rice will cook unevenly.

7 If you have a thin layer of rice at the top of your pot that does not get cooked all the way through, while the rest of the rice does, then your lid is not tight enough. Use aluminum foil between the pot and the lid next time around. Meanwhile, salvage your present situation by gently covering the partially cooked rice at the top with some fully cooked rice from the bottom. Add a tablespoon or two of water to the pot, cover tightly, this time using the foil, and cook for another 10 minutes over very low heat.

8 When removing cooked rice from the pot, use a large slotted spoon. Either scrape out the rice gently, layer by layer, or else ease the spoon gently into the rice, lift out as much as you can, put it on a plate and then break up any lumps by pressing lightly with the back of the spoon.

I have used two types of rice in this chapter, long-grain (which could be labeled "Patna" or "American long-grain") and basmati.

Basmati rice grows best in the foothills of the Himalaya Mountains, in both India and Pakistan. Actually, it too is a long-grain rice, only the grains are slender, delicate, naturally perfumed, and somewhat more expensive! The best basmati rice is aged for a year before it is sold. This aging increases its unusual, nutty aroma. It is not necessary to pick over and wash packaged rice (though washing will give it a better texture), but if you buy rice in burlap bags, you should look out for small stones and other impurities.

To pick it over, empty the rice onto one end of a large plate. Now work the rice from one side of the plate to the other, inspecting the grains carefully. Push any stones or other suspicious objects to one side.

Washing the grains: Put the picked rice in your largest bowl. Now fill the bowl with cold water and gently swirl the rice around it. The water will become cloudy with starch. Carefully pour the water away, holding back the rice with your free hand. Repeat five or six times, or as long as it takes for the water to remain reasonably clear.

Soaking: Fill up the bowl again, only this time leave the rice in the water for 20–30 minutes.

Now drain the rice in a strainer. It should sit in the strainer for at least 20 minutes to become fairly dry before you cook it.

If you use this method of preparation, combined with any of the various cooking methods given in the recipes, you will find that you need dramatically less water than you may have come to expect. Also your rice will have light, separated grains and will taste delicious.

The amazing thing about rice is that it can be cooked with almost any spice and combined with any vegetable, pulse, or meat. It is, perhaps, the world's most amenable grain.

plain, easy-to-cook, rice

Saaday chaaval

This is the quickest way of cooking American-style, packaged, long-grain rice. It requires no washing and no soaking and may be served with any food.

Serves 4 to 6

Long-grain rice measured to the 450 ml (2 cups) level in a glass measuring cup

750 ml (3 cups) water

1 teaspoon salt (optional)

15 g (1 tablespoon) unsalted butter (optional)

Combine the rice and water, and the salt and butter, if using, in a heavy pot and bring to a boil. Cover very tightly, turn heat to very, very low, and cook, undisturbed, for 25 minutes. Turn off the heat and let the pot rest, still covered and undisturbed, for another 5 minutes.

plain long-grain rice

Barhiya chaaval

This rice is slightly more elegant than the one in the preceding recipe mainly because it is washed and soaked before being cooked. These steps get rid of the starchy powder on the grains and help them to remain separate and unsplit.

Serves 4 to 6

Long-grain rice measured to the 450 ml (2 cups) level in a glass measuring cup

1.2 liters (5 cups) plus 600 ml (2^2/$_3$ cups) water

1 teaspoon salt

Put the rice in a bowl and wash in several changes of water. Drain. Soak in 1.2 liters (5 cups) water for 30 minutes. Drain thoroughly.

Put the drained rice, salt, and 600 ml (2^2/$_3$ cups) water in a heavy pot and bring to a boil. Cover with a very tight-fitting lid, turn heat to very, very low, and cook for 25 minutes. Take the rice pot off the heat and let it rest, still covered and undisturbed, for another 10 minutes.

south indian-style light, fluffy rice

Dakshini chaaval

In South India, rice is generally parboiled in a large, round-bottomed, narrow-necked utensil, with lots of water. When it is almost cooked, a cloth is tied to the mouth of the utensil and all the extra water drained out. (This water is later fed to the cows!) The pan is tilted so it lies on its belly over very low heat. A few live coals are placed on top of it as well to dry out the rice grains. Here is how the same rice may be made in a modern kitchen.

Serves 6

Long-grain rice measured to the 450 ml (2 cups) level in a glass measuring cup

2.75 liters (3 quarts) water

1 tablespoon salt (optional)

2–4 tablespoons unsalted butter (optional)

Preheat the oven to 150°C/300°F. Wash the rice in several changes of water and leave it to drain.

Fill a large pot with the water. Add the salt to it, if you wish, and bring to a rolling boil. Empty the rice into the boiling water in a steady stream, stirring as you do so. Let the water come to a boil again. Boil rapidly for 7 minutes. Drain the rice in a colander. Quickly put the rice in an ovenproof pan. Lay the butter, if using, over the rice, cover tightly, and put the pan in the oven for 35 minutes or until the rice is done. Mix gently before serving.

plain basmati rice

Basmati chaaval

I was brought up with this fine-grained rice. Now, as it has become quite expensive, it is served only at festive occasions and at parties.

Serves 6

Basmati rice measured to the 450 ml (2 cups) level in a glass measuring cup

1.2 liters (5 cups) plus 600 ml (2²/₃ cups) water

³/₄ teaspoon salt

1 tablespoon unsalted butter

Pick over the rice if necessary and put it in a bowl. Wash in several changes of water. Drain. Pour 1.2 liters (5 cups) fresh water over the rice and let it soak for 30 minutes. Drain thoroughly.

Combine the rice, salt, butter, and 600 ml (2²/₃ cups) water in a heavy-bottomed pot. Bring to a boil. Cover with a tight-fitting lid, turn heat to very low, and cook for 20 minutes. Lift the lid, mix gently but quickly with a fork, and cover again. Cook for another 5–10 minutes or until the rice is tender.

spiced basmati rice

Masaledar basmati

This is one of the finest – and most delicate – basmati rice dishes. It may be served with an Indian meal or with dishes such as roast lamb or grilled chicken.

Serves 6

Basmati rice measured to the 450 ml (2 cups) level in a glass measuring cup

1.2 liters (5 cups) water

3 tablespoons vegetable oil

1 small onion, peeled and finely chopped

½ fresh, hot green chili, finely chopped

½ teaspoon peeled, very finely chopped garlic

½ teaspoon *garam masala* (page 21)

1 teaspoon salt (a bit more if the stock is unsalted)

600 ml (2⅔ cups) chicken stock

Pick over the rice if necessary and put in a bowl. Wash in several changes of water. Drain. Pour 1.2 liters (5 cups) water over the rice and let it soak for 30 minutes. Leave to drain in a strainer for 20 minutes.

Put the oil in a heavy-bottomed pot and set over medium heat. When hot, put in the onion. Stir and fry until the onion bits have browned lightly. Add the rice, green chili, garlic, *garam masala,* and salt. Stir gently for 3–4 minutes until all the grains are coated with oil. If the rice begins to stick to the bottom of the pot, turn the heat down slightly. Now pour in the chicken stock and bring the rice to a boil. Cover with a very tight-fitting lid, turn heat to very, very low, and cook for 25 minutes.

If you prefer, you could put the pot in a preheated 170°C/325°F oven for 25 minutes.

simple buttery rice with onion

Pyaz wali basmati chaaval

This simple method of cooking rice makes it extremely versatile. You could serve it with Indian and Western meals.

Serves 6

4 tablespoons unsalted butter

1 medium onion, peeled and chopped

Long-grain rice measured to the 450 ml (2 cups) level in a glass measuring cup

1 teaspoon salt

750 ml (3 cups) water

Melt the butter in a heavy pot over medium heat. When hot, put in the onion. Stir and sauté them until they are almost translucent. Do not let them brown in the slightest. Put in the rice and the salt. Stir and sauté gently for a minute. Pour in the water and bring to a boil. Cover tightly, turn heat to very, very low, and let the rice cook for 25 minutes.

rice with yellow split peas

Khili hui khichri

Khichri is of ancient origin. I have read descriptions of it written by travelers who came to India as long as a thousand years ago. *Khichri* probably predates even these early travelers. It consists, basically, of rice and pulses cooked together and is served in most Indian homes in one of two forms, the "wet," porridgelike version and the "dry," grainy version. The recipe here is for the "dry" *khichri,* which my mother always referred to as *khili hui khichri* or "the *khichri* that has bloomed." This has the consistency of well-prepared rice. You could serve it with Kashmiri Lamb Stew (page 63) and an onion relish.

Serves 6

50 g (2 oz) yellow split peas, picked over, washed, and drained

450 ml (15 fl oz) plus 1.2 liters (2 pints) water

Long-grain rice measured to the 450 ml (15 fl oz) level in a glass measuring cup

3 tablespoons *ghee* (page 28) or vegetable oil

¹/₂ teaspoon cumin seeds

¹/₂ teaspoon *garam masala* (page 21)

1 teaspoon salt, or to taste

4 tablespoons finely chopped, fresh green coriander (parsley may be substituted)

600 ml (1 pint) chicken stock (water may be substituted)

Soak the split peas in 450 ml (15 fl oz) water for 3 hours. Drain. Wash the rice in several changes of water and drain. Soak in 1.2 liters (2 pints) water for 1 hour. Drain.

Put the *ghee* or oil in a heavy pot and set over medium heat. When hot, put in the cumin seeds. Stir them around for a few seconds. Now put in the drained split peas and rice. Stir and sauté for 2–3 minutes or until the grains are coated with the *ghee*. Add the *garam masala*, salt, and fresh coriander or parsley. Stir and sauté for another minute or so. Add the chicken stock or water and bring to a boil. Cover tightly, turn heat to very, very low, and cook for 25 minutes. Turn off the heat and let the pot sit, covered and undisturbed, for another 10 minutes.

Stir gently with a slotted spoon or fork before serving.

rice and peas

Tahiri

This rice dish is flavored, very mildly, with cumin seeds, making it suitable for almost any kind of meal.

Serves 6

Long-grain rice measured to the 450 ml (2 cups) level in a glass measuring cup

1.2 liters (5 cups) plus 600 ml ($2^2/_3$ cups) water

3 tablespoons vegetable oil

1 teaspoon cumin seeds

1 medium onion, peeled and finely chopped

150–175 g ($1^1/_4$ cups) fresh, shelled peas (frozen, defrosted peas may be substituted)

1 teaspoon salt

Wash the rice in several changes of water and drain. Put the rice in a bowl. Add 1.2 liters (5 cups) water and soak for 30 minutes. Drain.

Put the oil in a heavy pot and set over medium heat. When hot, put in the cumin seeds. Stir them about for 3 seconds. Now put in the chopped onion. Stir and fry them until they get flecked with brown spots. Add the peas, rice, and salt. Stir and sauté gently for 3–4 minutes or until the peas and rice are coated with oil. Add 600 ml ($2^2/_3$ cups) water and bring to a boil. Cover very tightly, turn heat to very, very low, and cook for 25 minutes. Turn off the heat and let the pot sit, covered and undisturbed, for another 5 minutes. Stir gently before serving.

vegetable pullao

Sabzi pullao

Sometimes, when I want an all-vegetarian meal, I serve this pullao with Black-eyed
Beans with Mushrooms (page 174) and a yogurt dish. It can, of course, be served with
any meat.

Serves 6

Long-grain rice measured to the 450 ml
(2 cups) level in a glass measuring cup

1.2 liters (5 cups) plus 600 ml
(2²/₃ cups) water

1 medium potato, peeled

¹/₂ medium-sized carrot, about
40 g (1¹/₂ oz), peeled

12–16 fresh green beans

4 tablespoons vegetable oil

1 teaspoon cumin seeds

1¹/₄ teaspoons salt

¹/₂ teaspoon ground turmeric

1 teaspoon ground cumin

1 teaspoon ground coriander

¹/₄ teaspoon cayenne pepper

¹/₂ fresh, hot green chili, finely chopped

2 tablespoons very finely chopped cilantro

¹/₂ teaspoon peeled, very finely
grated fresh ginger

1 clove garlic, peeled and
mashed to a pulp

Put the rice in a bowl and wash in several changes of water. Drain. Add
1.2 liters (5 cups) water and leave to soak for 30 minutes. Drain and leave in
a strainer for 20 minutes.

Cut the potatoes and carrot into 5 mm (¹/₄ inch) dice. Trim the green beans and
cut, crosswise, at 5 mm (¹/₄ inch) intervals.

Put the oil in a heavy pot over medium heat. When hot, put in the cumin seeds.
Let them sizzle for 5–6 seconds. Now put in the potato, carrot, and green beans.
Stir and sauté for a minute. Turn the heat to medium-low and add the drained
rice, salt, turmeric, ground cumin, ground coriander, cayenne, green chili,
cilantro, ginger, and garlic. Stir and sauté the rice for 2–3 minutes. Add 600 ml
(1 pint) water and bring to a boil. Cover very tightly, turn heat to very, very low,
and cook for 25 minutes. Turn off the heat and let the pot sit, covered and
undisturbed, for another 10 minutes.

mushroom pullao

Khumbi pullao

My mother used to make this dish with morel mushrooms. Wild morels can be bought in specialty produce markets in April and the season can last through June. Just slice them in half, lengthwise. I tend to make this dish quite often and find myself using the more easily available cultivated mushrooms. Cultivated morels appear sporadically throughout the year. It is still a superb dish and may be served with almost any meat dish in this book. You could also serve it with a roast leg of lamb or with lamb chops.

Serves 6

Long-grain rice measured to the 450 ml (2 cups) level in a glass measuring cup

1.2 liters (5 cups) plus 600 ml ($2^2/_3$ cups) water

150 g (5 oz) mushrooms

1 small onion, peeled

3 tablespoons vegetable oil

1 clove garlic, peeled and finely chopped

$^1/_2$ teaspoon peeled, finely grated fresh ginger

$^1/_4$ teaspoon *garam masala* (page 21)

1 teaspoon salt

Wash the rice in several changes of water and drain. Put the rice in a bowl. Add 1.2 liters (5 cups) water and soak for 30 minutes. Drain.

Wipe the mushrooms with a dampened cloth or paper towel. Cut the mushrooms, from the caps down to the stems, into 3 mm (1/8 inch) thick slices. Cut the onion in half, lengthwise, and then crosswise into very thin slices.

Put the oil in a heavy pot and set over medium heat. When hot, put in the onion and garlic. Stir and fry for about 2 minutes or until the onion pieces begin to turn brown at the edges. Put in the mushrooms and stir for another 2 minutes. Now put in the rice, ginger, *garam masala,* and salt. Turn heat to medium low. Stir and sauté the rice for 2 minutes. Pour in 600 ml ($2^2/_3$ cups) water and bring to a boil. Cover very tightly, turn heat to very, very low, and cook for 25 minutes. Turn off the heat and let the pan sit, covered and undisturbed, for another 5 minutes.

aromatic yellow rice

Peelay chaaval

You may use either basmati rice or American long-grain rice for this recipe. The yellow color, here, comes from ground turmeric. I like to serve it with Chicken in a Red Sweet Pepper Sauce (page 101) and Gujerati-style Green Beans (page 131) just to get a wonderful contrast of bright colors.

Serves 6

Long-grain or basmati rice measured to the 450 ml (2 cups) level in a glass measuring cup

1.2 liters (5 cups) plus 600 ml (2²/₃ cups) water

1¼ teaspoons salt

³/₄ teaspoon ground turmeric

3–4 cloves

2.5 cm (1 inch) cinnamon stick

3 bay leaves

3 tablespoons unsalted butter, cut into small pats

Put the rice in a bowl and wash in several changes of water. Drain. Pour 1.2 liters (5 cups) fresh water over the rice and let it soak for 30 minutes. Drain the rice in a strainer.

Combine the drained rice, 600 ml (2²/₃ cups) water, salt, turmeric, cloves, cinnamon, and bay leaves in a heavy pot and bring to a boil. Cover with a tight-fitting lid, turn heat to very, very low, and cook for 25 minutes. Let the pot rest, covered and undisturbed, for 10 minutes.

Add the small pats of butter to the rice and mix them in very gently using a fork.

Remove the whole spices before serving.

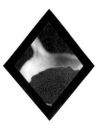

sweet yellow rice

Meetha pullao

This wonderful, shining rice may be eaten by itself, with hot, spicy Indian dishes or even with other foods such as baked ham and roast turkey or goose.

Saffron does give this dish a very special flavor but if you are on a tight budget and find saffron a bit too expensive, just leave it (and the milk) out and increase the yellow food coloring to 1 teaspoon.

Serves 4

$^1/_2$ teaspoon saffron threads

2 tablespoons warm milk

Basmati rice measured to the 250 ml (1 cup) level in a glass measuring cup

1.2 liters (5 cups) plus 300 ml (1$^1/_4$ cups) water

4 tablespoons *ghee* (page 28) or unsalted butter

4 cardamom pods

2.5 cm (1 inch) cinnamon stick

$^1/_4$ teaspoon liquid yellow food coloring

$^1/_2$ teaspoon salt

2 tablespoons blanched, slivered almonds

1 tablespoon golden raisins

6 tablespoons sugar, depending upon taste

Put the saffron in a small heavy frying pan set over medium heat. Stir it until the threads turn a few shades darker. Put the milk in a small cup and crumble the saffron into it. Set it aside for 3 hours.

Wash the rice in several changes of water and drain it. Leave it to soak in 1.2 liters (5 cups) water for 30 minutes. Drain for 20 minutes.

Preheat the oven to 150°C/300°F.

Put the *ghee* or butter in a wide, heavy, ovenproof pot and set over medium heat. When hot, put in the cardamom pods and cinnamon. Stir them for a second. Now put in the rice. Stir and sauté the rice gently for about 3 minutes, turning the heat down slightly if it begins to burn. Add 300 ml (1$^1/_4$ cups) water, the yellow coloring, and the salt. Turn the heat back to medium. Gently stir and cook the rice until all the water is absorbed. Put in the saffron milk, almonds, raisins, and sugar. Stir to mix, cover very tightly, and put the pot in the oven for 30 minutes. Remove from oven and stir to mix.

Remove the cardamom pods and cinnamon before serving. If liked, silver *varak* (page 24) can be placed on the rice with a few raisins and nuts on top.

lamb and rice casserole
Mughlai lamb biryani

Biryanis are grand, festive casseroles in which partially cooked rice is layered over cooked meat. Orange saffron milk is dribbled over the top, thereby coloring some grains yellow while leaving others white, and the dish set to bake in a slow oven. As it cooks, the *biryani* gets quite perfumed with saffron.

Saffron is expensive and many people, even in India, use yellow food coloring as a substitute. Just use 1 teaspoon yellow liquid food coloring diluted with 1 teaspoon water instead of the saffron and warm milk. Soaking the rice in salted water for 3–24 hours, is an ancient trick the Persians used to get rice grains as white – and as separate from each other – as possible.

A *biryani* is really a meal in itself and may be eaten with just a yogurt dish, such as Yogurt with Eggplant (page 212), and a relish, such as my Tomato, Onion, and Cilantro Relish (page 215). However, *biryanis* are generally served at feasts and banquets when it would not be at all amiss to serve these condiments *as well as* Chicken in a Red Sweet Pepper Sauce (page 101) and Cauliflower with Onion and Tomato (page 142).

Serves 6

Long-grain rice measured to the 450 ml
(2 cups) level in a glass measuring cup

2 liters (9 cups) plus 3 tablespoons
plus 150 ml (2/3 cup) plus 3.6 liters
(15 cups) water

About 3 tablespoons salt

1 teaspoon saffron threads

2 tablespoons warm milk

3 medium-sized onions, peeled

4 cloves garlic, peeled

2 cm (3/4 inch) cube fresh ginger,
peeled and coarsely chopped

4 tablespoons blanched, slivered almonds

13 tablespoons vegetable oil

3 tablespoons golden raisins

750 g (1½ lb) boned lamb from the
shoulder, cut into 2.5 cm (1 inch) cubes

250 ml (1 cup) plain yogurt

5–6 cloves

½ teaspoon black peppercorns

½ teaspoon cardamom seeds

1 teaspoon cumin seeds

1 teaspoon coriander seeds

2.5 cm (1 inch) cinnamon stick

About 1/6 nutmeg

¼ teaspoon cayenne pepper

2 tablespoons unsalted butter, cut
into 8 pieces

3 hard-boiled eggs, peeled and
at room temperature

Wash the rice in several changes of water. Drain it and put it in a large bowl. Add 2 liters (9 cups) water and 1 tablespoon of the salt. Mix and soak for 3 hours.

Put the saffron threads in a small, heavy (preferably cast-iron) frying pan set over medium heat. Toss the threads about until they turn a few shades darker. Put the warm milk in a small cup. Crumble the saffron into the warm milk and soak for 3 hours.

Cut 2 of the onions in half, lengthwise, and then cut the halves into fine rings. Set these aside. Chop the remaining onion very coarsely. Put this chopped onion, garlic, ginger, 2 tablespoons of the almonds, and 3 tablespoons water into the container of an electric blender. Blend until you have a paste.

Put 6 tablespoons of the oil in a 25 cm (10 inch), preferably nonstick, frying pan and set over medium-high heat. When hot, put in the onion rings. Stir and fry them until they are brown and crisp. Remove them with a slotted spoon and spread them out on a plate lined with paper towels.

Put the raisins into the same oil. Remove them as soon as they turn plump – which happens immediately. Put the raisins in another plate lined with paper towels. Put the remaining 2 tablespoons almonds into the oil. Stir and fry them until they are golden. Remove them with a slotted spoon and spread them out beside the raisins. Set aside for use as the garnish.

Now put the meat cubes, a few at a time, into the same hot oil and brown them on all sides. As each batch gets done, put in a bowl.

Add the remaining 7 tablespoons of the oil to the frying pan and turn heat to medium. When hot, put in the onion-garlic-ginger-almond paste from the blender. Fry, stirring all the time, until the paste turns a medium-brown color. If it sticks slightly to the bottom of the pan, sprinkle in a little water and keep stirring. Return the meat and any accumulated juices to the pan. Add the yogurt, 1 tablespoon at a time, stirring well between each addition. Now put in 1¼ teaspoons of the salt and 150 ml (2/3 cup) water. Mix and bring to a simmer. Cover, turn heat to low, and simmer for 30 minutes.

While the meat is cooking, put the cloves, peppercorns, cardamom seeds, cumin seeds, coriander seeds, cinnamon, and nutmeg into the container of a spice grinder or a clean coffee grinder. Grind finely.

When the meat has cooked for 30 minutes, add all the spices from the spice grinder as well as the cayenne and mix well. Cover again and continue to cook on low heat for another 30 minutes. Remove cover, raise heat to medium, and cook, stirring all the time, until you have about 200 ml (1¹/₄ cups) thick sauce left at the bottom of the pan. Turn off the heat and spoon off as much grease as possible. The meat should be pretty well cooked by now.

Spread out the meat and sauce in the bottom of a heavy casserole. Cover and keep warm.

Preheat the oven to 150°C/300°F.

Bring 3.6 liters (15 cups) water to a rolling boil in a large pot. Add 1½ tablespoons salt to it. Drain the rice and rinse it off under running water. Slowly, scatter the rice into the boiling water. Bring to a boil again and boil rapidly for exactly 6 minutes. Then drain the rice.

Work fast now. Put the rice on top of the meat, piling it up in the shape of a hill. Take a chopstick or the handle of a long spoon and make a 2.5 cm (1 inch) wide hole going down like a well from the peak of the rice hill to its bottom. Dribble the saffron milk in streaks along the sides of the hill. Lay the pieces of butter on the sides of the hill and scatter 2 tablespoons of the browned onions over it as well. Cover first with aluminum foil, sealing the edges well, and then with a lid. Bake in the oven for 1 hour. Remove from the oven. If left in a warm place, this rice will stay hot for 30 minutes.

Just before you get ready to serve, quarter the eggs, lengthwise. Mix the contents of the rice pot gently. Serve the *biryani* on a warmed platter, garnished with the eggs, remaining browned onions, raisins, and almonds.

We like to perk up our meals in India with a variety of condiments. Their function, apart from teasing the palate with their sharp contrasts of sweet, sour, hot, and salty flavors, is to balance out the meal with added protein and vitamins.

Sometimes, these condiments can be quite simple — cucumber wedges seasoned quickly with salt, pepper, cayenne, and lemon juice or chopped-up onions and tomatoes. At other times we can serve pickles that have taken weeks or months to mature. Some condiments, such as the Cilantro Chutney or the Gujerati Carrot Salad, should be eaten within 48 hours. Others, such as the Apple, Peach, and Apricot Chutney and the Cauliflower and White Radish Pickle, may be kept for a year.

Yogurt relishes fall into another category. They can be condiments or they can be substantial dishes by themselves. Almost any herb or vegetable can be put into yogurts, from mint to potatoes. Whenever I am serving an all-Indian meal, I nearly always serve a yogurt relish because it provides a cooling contrast.

relishes, chutneys, and pickles

plain yogurt

Dahi

Yogurt is used in India for marinating meats – it tenderizes them – as a tart, creamy flavoring and as an ingredient for sauces. As it is rich in protein, it is also eaten at almost every meal, either plain or mixed with seasonings and vegetables. It is a food that is easy to digest, far easier than milk. It is also considered a food that "settles" the stomach, especially when combined with plain rice.

Naturally, few respectable Indian homes are ever without it. Most of the time it is made at home, although it can be bought from the bazaar as well.

To make yogurt at home, you need milk, either whole or fat-free, and some "starter." This "starter" is a few tablespoons of borrowed, leftover, or bought yogurt. You also need a warm temperature that hovers between 30°–38°C (85°–100°F). This is the temperature at which yogurt sets best. As this is not normally room temperature, it has to be approximated. You could put the yogurt in a warm cupboard near the water heater or in the oven of a stove with a pilot light. The yogurt bowl is also quite amenable to being wrapped in a blanket. I frequently resort to the blanket method.

1 liter (1 quart) milk
2 tablespoons plain yogurt

Bring the milk to a boil in a heavy pot. As soon as the milk begins to rise, remove the pot from the stove. Let the milk cool to anywhere between 38° and 43°C (100–110°F). It should feel warm to the touch. If a film forms over the top, stir it in.

Put the yogurt in a 1.2 liter (5 cup) stainless steel or nonmetallic bowl and beat it with a whisk until it is smooth and creamy. Slowly add the warm milk, a little bit at a time, and stir as you do so. Cover the bowl and then wrap it in an old blanket or shawl without tilting it. Set it aside in a warm place free of drafts for 6–8 hours, or until the yogurt has set.

Store the yogurt in a refrigerator. It should stay fresh for 4–5 days.

yogurt with cucumber and mint

Kheere ka raita

Here is a cooling yogurt dish that can be served with all Indian meals. It also makes an excellent snack that can be stored in the refrigerator and then taken out whenever someone comes in complaining of being tired, hot, and hungry.

Serves 6

600 ml (2²/₃ cups) plain yogurt

1 small cucumber, peeled and coarsely grated

2 tablespoons finely chopped, fresh mint

¹/₂ teaspoon ground, roasted cumin seeds (page 20)

¹/₄ teaspoon cayenne pepper

1 teaspoon salt

Freshly ground black pepper

Put the yogurt in a bowl. Beat lightly with a fork or whisk until smooth and creamy.

Add all the other ingredients and mix. Cover and refrigerate until ready to eat.

yogurt with walnuts and cilantro

Akhrote ka raita

Another cooling, nourishing dish. It may be eaten by itself or served with Indian meals.

Serves 6

600 ml (2²/₃ cups) plain yogurt

2 tablespoons finely chopped cilantro

¹/₂ fresh, hot green chili,
very finely chopped

About ¹/₂ teaspoon salt, or to taste

Freshly ground black pepper

1 scallion, very finely sliced

65 g (¹/₂ cup) shelled walnuts, broken up,
roughly, into 1–2 cm (¹/₃–¹/₂ inch) pieces

Put the yogurt in a bowl. Beat lightly with a fork or a whisk until it is smooth and creamy. Add all the other ingredients. Stir to mix.

yogurt with eggplant

Baigan ka raita

Here is a soothing, cooling, and exceedingly simple way to serve eggplant. I like to serve this with Delhi-style Lamb Cooked with Potatoes (page 73), Gujerati-style Green Beans (page 131), and either rice or an Indian bread.

Serves 6

1 medium-sized (550 g/1¼ lb) eggplant, peeled and cut into 2.5 cm (1 inch) cubes

600 ml (2⅔ cups) plain yogurt

¾ teaspoon salt, or to taste

Freshly ground black pepper

⅛ teaspoon cayenne pepper (optional)

1 scallion, washed and cut into paper-thin rounds all the way up its green section

1 tablespoon finely chopped, fresh mint

A few mint leaves for garnishing

Bring water in the bottom part of a steaming utensil to the boil. (If you do not have a steaming utensil, set a colander inside a large pot. Pour water into the pot in such a way that it stays just below the lowest part of the colander. Bring this water to a boil.)

Put the eggplant cubes into the steamer section of your steaming utensil (or into the colander), cover, and steam over high heat for 10 minutes. Make sure that your boiling water does not run out.

While the eggplant is steaming, put the yogurt into a bowl and beat it lightly with a fork or a whisk until it is smooth and creamy. Add the salt, black pepper, cayenne, if using, scallion, and mint to it. Mix with a fork.

Lift out the steamed eggplant pieces and mash with a fork. Spread out the eggplant on a plate and leave to cool somewhat (or else the yogurt would curdle).

Fold the eggplant into the yogurt and garnish with mint leaves.

gujerati-style yogurt with potatoes

Batata nu raita

This is an Indian potato salad except that we use seasoned yogurt as a dressing instead of mayonnaise or a vinaigrette. In order to make the yogurt very thick and creamy, it is generally hung up in a cheesecloth for an hour. You may omit this step if you are in a rush. You will, of course, end up with a more "flowing" sauce, rather than one that clings to the potatoes. It may be served with Minced Meat with Peas (page 62) and an Indian bread.

Serves 4

2 large potatoes
425 ml (2 cups) plain yogurt
½ teaspoon salt
Freshly ground black pepper
2 tablespoons vegetable oil
1 teaspoon cumin seeds
⅛ teaspoon cayenne pepper, or to taste
Optional garnish: 1 tablespoon finely chopped cilantro or parsley

Boil the potatoes in their jackets. Drain them and let them cool for at least an hour.

Set a strainer over a bowl and line it with a 38–40 cm (15–16 inch) square of doubled cheesecloth, muslin, or a clean dish towel. Put the yogurt into the cheesecloth. Now bring the 4 corners of the cheesecloth together. Use one of the corners to tie the cheesecloth into a bundle. Hang this bundle somewhere so it can drip for an hour. I usually hang it from the tap in my sink. Do not squeeze the cheesecloth. Just let it drip.

Empty the yogurt into a bowl. Add about ¼ teaspoon of the salt and some black pepper. Beat lightly with a fork or a whisk until the yogurt is smooth and creamy. Taste for seasonings.

Peel the potatoes and cut them into 2 cm (¾ inch) dice. Put the oil in a frying pan (nonstick is best) and set over medium heat. When hot, put in the cumin seeds. Let the cumin seeds sizzle for 3–4 seconds. Now put in the diced potatoes, about ⅓ teaspoon salt, some black pepper and the cayenne. Stir and cook the potatoes for about 4 minutes. Taste a potato piece for salt and other seasonings. You may make this dish as hot as you like. Take the frying pan off the heat and let the potatoes cool for 5 minutes. Pour the contents of the frying pan – oil, spices, and potatoes – into the bowl with the yogurt.

Stir to mix and garnish the salad, if you like, with cilantro or parsley.

tomato, onion, and cilantro relish

Cachumber

This tasty relish complements almost all Indian meals.

Serves 4 to 6

2 medium tomatoes

1 medium onion, peeled

4 heaped tablespoons chopped cilantro (parsley may be substituted)

¾ teaspoon salt

2 tablespoons lemon juice

½ teaspoon cayenne pepper

½ teaspoon ground, roasted cumin seeds (page 20)

Cut the tomatoes and onion into 5 mm (¼ inch) dice and put them in a smallish, nonmetallic serving bowl. Add the cilantro or parsley, salt, lemon juice, cayenne, and cumin seeds, and mix.

apple, peach, and apricot chutney

Sev, aroo, aur kubani ki chutney

This superb, fruity, sweet-and-sour chutney has the thick consistency of a preserve and may be bottled and kept for long periods. Those who like their chutney very hot can add up to 1½ teaspoons cayenne pepper. It may be served with all Indian meals as well as with pork chops and ham.

Makes about 750 ml (3 cups)

½ kg (4–5) sour cooking apples, peeled, cored, and coarsely chopped

100 g (¾ cup) dried peaches, quartered

100 g (¾ cup) dried apricots

50 g (½ cup) golden raisins

6 cloves garlic, peeled and mashed to a pulp

Two 2.5 cm (1 inch) cubes fresh ginger, peeled and finely grated

400 ml (1¾ cups) white wine vinegar

385 g (2⅓ cups) granulated sugar

2 teaspoons salt

½ teaspoon cayenne pepper

Combine all the ingredients in a heavy stainless steel or nonstick pot and bring to a boil. Turn heat to medium-low and cook, keeping up a fairly vigorous simmer, for about 30 minutes or until you have a thick, jamlike consistency. Stir frequently and turn the heat down slightly when the chutney thickens as it could stick to the bottom of the pan.

Let the chutney cool. It will thicken some more as it cools. Pour into a clean jar and cover with a nonmetallic lid. Store in a cool place or keep in the refrigerator.

gujerati carrot salad

Gajar ka salad

This simple, lightly spiced, easy-to-make salad may be served with Indian meals — or with something as Western as grilled sausages! There are many variations to it that you might like to try out on your family and friends. You could, for example, leave out the lemon juice. This highlights the natural sweetness of the carrots. Or you could add 2 tablespoons raisins that you should soak in hot water for 2–3 hours first.

Serves 4

5 carrots, trimmed, peeled, and coarsely grated
¼ teaspoon salt
2 tablespoons vegetable oil
1 tablespoon black mustard seeds
2 teaspoons lemon juice

In a bowl, toss the grated carrots with the salt. Put the oil in a very small saucepan and set over medium heat.

When the oil is very hot, put in the mustard seeds. As soon as the mustard seeds begin to pop — this takes just a few seconds — pour the contents of the saucepan — oil and seeds — over the carrots.

Add the lemon juice and toss.

You may serve this salad at room temperature or cold.

carrot and onion salad

Gajar aur pyaz ka salad

This salad is made with the deep red, beetlike "bleeding" carrot that is found in North India during the winter months. I have substituted the ordinary orange carrot. It may be served with nearly all Indian meals.

Serves 6

3 carrots, about 225 g (½ lb) in all
1 medium onion, peeled
¾ teaspoon salt
Freshly ground black pepper
4 teaspoons lemon juice
⅛ –¼ teaspoon cayenne pepper
½ teaspoon peeled, finely grated fresh ginger

Peel the carrots and cut them, crosswise and at a diagonal, into 3 mm (⅛ inch) thick oval slices. Cut the slices, lengthwise, into 3 mm (⅛ inch) wide strips. Halve the onion, lengthwise, and then cut it crosswise into 3 mm (⅛ inch) thick slices.

Bring the water in a medium saucepan to a rolling boil. Throw in the carrots. Bring to a boil again. Boil rapidly for 2 seconds only. Drain the carrots immediately and rinse them under cold, running water. Drain again.

Combine the carrots, onion, salt, black pepper, lemon juice, cayenne, and ginger. Stir to mix.

This salad may be served as soon as it is made or several hours later. It may be served at room temperature or cold.

spicy cucumber wedges

Kheere ke tukray

These wedges (pictured opposite) are refreshing and deliciously crunchy and may be served with any Indian meal. It is best to prepare them at the last minute, just before you sit down to eat.

Serves 4

2 medium cucumbers
(about 25 cm/10 inches)

1/3 teaspoon salt

1/8 teaspoon cayenne pepper

Freshly ground black pepper

1/3 teaspoon ground, roasted cumin seeds
(page 20)

Juice of 3/4 lemon (approx.)

Peel the cucumbers and cut them in half, crosswise. Now cut each half into 4 sections, lengthwise. Arrange the wedges on a plate. Sprinkle the salt, cayenne, black pepper, ground, roasted cumin seeds, and lemon juice over them. **Serve immediately.**

cilantro chutney

Hare dhaniye ki chutney

This is the kind of chutney that is made fresh in our homes every day. We eat small amounts – 1–2 teaspoons – with our meals, just as you might eat mustard with meats. It also serves as an excellent dip for snacks such as *samosas*.

Serves 4–6

75 g (3 cups) cilantro (weight without lower stems and roots), coarsely chopped

1/2–1 fresh, hot green chili,
coarsely chopped

11/2 tablespoons lemon juice

1/2 teaspoon salt

1/2 teaspoon ground, roasted cumin seeds
(page 20)

Freshly ground black pepper

Combine all the ingredients in the container of an electric blender. Blend, pushing down with a rubber spatula several times, until you have a paste. Empty the paste into a small glass or other nonmetallic bowl.

cauliflower and white radish pickle

Phool gobi aur mooli ka achaar

This is one of the simplest Indian pickles. It does take several days to mature, so you have to be patient. Small amounts of it may be served at all Indian meals. You may substitute turnip slices for the white radish in this recipe. The mustard seeds and oil, however, are essential. I heat the mustard oil before I use it in the pickle, because this process transforms it from a pungent oil to a sweet one.

Makes enough to fill a 1 liter (1 quart) jar

225 g (^{1}/$_2$ head) cauliflower
5–6 white radishes
(weight without leaves)
4 teaspoons black mustard seeds
120 ml (4 fl oz) mustard oil
2 teaspoons salt
^{1}/$_2$ teaspoon ground turmeric
^{1}/$_2$–1 teaspoon cayenne pepper

Cut the cauliflower into thin florets that are 2.5–4 cm (1–1^1/$_2$ inches) across at the head, 7mm–1 cm ([^{1}/$_3$–^{1}/$_2$ inch) wide, and 4–5 cm (1^1/$_2$–2 inches) in length. Peel the radish and cut it into 7 mm (^{1}/$_3$ inch) thick rounds. If the diameter of the slices is more than 2.5 cm (1 inch), halve or quarter the slices.

Grind the mustard seeds coarsely in a coffee grinder or spice grinder.

Put the oil in a small saucepan or frying pan and set over medium heat. As soon as it gets very, very hot, turn off the heat and let it cool. (Remember to take very great care with hot oil – stand over the oil as it cools.)

Put the cut vegetables in a bowl. Add the ground mustard seeds, salt, turmeric, and cayenne. Mix well. Add the oil and mix again. Empty the contents of the bowl into a 1.2 liter (5 cup) glass or ceramic jar and cover with a nonmetallic lid. For the next few days, put the jar in a warm, sunny spot in the daytime and, if that spot is outdoors, bring the jar in at night. This pickle may take 4–5 days to mature in the summer and about 8 days in the winter.

Make sure you shake the jar at least 3–4 times a day. When the pickle is sour enough for your liking, it is ready. You may store it in a cool part of the kitchen.

onion relish

Pyaz ka laccha

This is one of those relishes that may be served with almost every Indian meal. It may be familiar to you from Indian restaurants where it is sometimes described as onion chutney.

Serves 4

1 medium onion, peeled
³/₄ teaspoon salt
4 teaspoons lemon juice
¹/₄ teaspoon paprika (the redder in color, the better)
¹/₈ teaspoon cayenne pepper

Cut the onion, crosswise, into paper-thin rings. Put the rings into a bowl. Add all the other ingredients. Toss and mix. Set aside for 30 minutes (or more) before eating, in order to let the flavors blend.

crisp, browned onions

Bhuni hui pyaz

These onions, when sprinkled over cooked foods, serve as a flavorful garnish. When crumbled and added to sauces for meats and vegetables they provide a distinctive texture, taste, and color.

Makes enough to fill a 300 ml (²/₃ cup) jar

2 medium onions, peeled
Vegetable oil for sautéing

Cut the onions in half, lengthwise. Now cut them crosswise into very, very thin, even slices.

Heat about 1 cm (¹/₂ inch) oil in a 20–23 cm (8–9 inch) frying pan over medium heat. When hot, put in all the onions. Stir and fry the onions until they turn reddish brown in color. Remove them with a slotted spoon and spread them out on a plate lined with paper towels. As the onions cool, they should turn quite crisp. They may be eaten the same day or else stored in a tightly closed container for a few days.

Everyday meals in India generally end with fresh fruit – mangoes, pineapples, oranges, apples, pears, bananas, guavas, cherries, melons – whatever happens to be in season. Fruit is refreshing and cleansing – and a perfect conclusion to a spicy meal.

In our family, my mother always peeled and cut the smaller fruit for all of us at the table. A plate was passed around and we took what we wanted. Larger, messier fruit, such as watermelons, were cut in the kitchen before the meal and left to cool in the refrigerator.

Desserts and candies are usually reserved for festive occasions. A wedding banquet invariably brings forth large vats filled with *kulfi* – Indian ice cream – and at religious festivals some variety of *halva* is nearly always served.

sweets

drunken orange slices

Sharabi narangi

There could be nothing simpler than this dessert. All that it requires are good oranges, some cinnamon, and Grand Marnier. It is just perfect after a spicy Indian meal.

Serves 4

4 good, juicy oranges
¹⁄₃ teaspoon ground cinnamon
120 ml (¹⁄₂ cup) Grand Marnier

Peel the whole oranges, leaving no white pith. Slice into 5 mm (¹⁄₄ inch) thick rounds and arrange in a bowl in overlapping slices, sprinkling a little cinnamon over each layer. Cover and refrigerate. Just before serving, pour the Grand Marnier evenly over the top.

semolina halva

Sooji ka halva

This very light, fluffy *halva* may be eaten as a snack or at the end of a meal. It is very popular with children.

Serves 6

600 ml (1¹/₄ cups) water

5 tablespoons vegetable oil or *ghee* (page 28)

3 tablespoons slivered, blanched almonds

300 g (2 cups) fine-grained semolina

165 g (³/₄ cup) sugar

2–3 tablespoons golden raisins

¹/₄ teaspoon finely crushed cardamom seeds (use a pestle and mortar for this)

Put 600 ml (1¹/₄ cups) water to boil in a saucepan. Once it comes to a rolling boil, turn the heat down to very low and let the pan sit on the back of the stove.

Put the oil or *ghee* in a large, preferably nonstick, frying pan and set over medium heat. When hot, put in the almonds. Stir and fry them until they turn golden. Take them out with a slotted spoon and leave them to drain on paper towels. Put the semolina into the same oil. Turn the heat to medium-low. Now stir and sauté the semolina for 8–10 minutes or until it turns a warm, golden color. Do not let it brown.

Add the sugar and stir it in.

Very slowly, begin to pour the boiling water into the saucepan. Keep stirring as you do so. Take a good 2 minutes to do this. When all the water has been added, turn the heat to low. Stir and cook the *halva* for 5 minutes. Add the raisins, almonds, and crushed cardamom seeds. Stir and cook the *halva* for another 5 minutes.

This *halva* may be served hot, warm, or at room temperature.

vermicelli pudding

Seviyan ki kheer

In India, we use a very thin, delicate vermicelli known as *seviyan* to make this pudding. Since this is available only in Indian stores, I have worked out a recipe for the vermicelli that can be found in most supermarkets.

Serves 6 to 8

4 tablespoons unsalted butter

75 g (2 cups) vermicelli, broken into 5 cm (2 inch) lengths

1.5 liters (6¼ cups) hot milk

¼ teaspoon cardamom seeds, crushed to a powder in a mortar

2 tablespoons golden raisins

3 tablespoons chopped almonds

100 g (½ cup plus 2 tablespoons) sugar, or to taste

2 tablespoons finely chopped pistachios (use more almonds as a substitute)

Melt the butter in a heavy pot over medium-low heat. Put in the vermicelli. Stay watchful now. Stir and fry the vermicelli until the pieces turn golden-brown. This happens rather suddenly. Some pieces will be darker than others. That is to be expected. Pour in the hot milk and bring to a simmer. Now adjust the heat to medium-low or whatever temperature keeps the milk simmering vigorously without letting it boil over. Add the cardamom seeds, raisins, and almonds.

Let the milk simmer vigorously for about 20 minutes. Stir frequently during this period. Add the sugar and cook another 5 minutes. You should now have about 1.2 liters (5 cups) of pudding or a bit less.

Pour the pudding into a bowl and allow to turn lukewarm. Stir a few times as this happens. A skin will form on the top. Just stir it in. Pour the lukewarm pudding into a single serving bowl or into several individual bowls. Garnish with the pistachios, cover with plastic wrap, and refrigerate.

Serve cold.

ice cream with nuts

Kulfi

As far as I can remember, we never made *kulfi* at home. This may well have been because it was served always to hundreds of people at wedding banquets. Only a professional *kulfi-wallah* could be entrusted with such a monstrous task. Orders were placed with him weeks in advance. On the day of the banquet, he arrived with assistants, usually his sons and brothers, carrying enormous earthenware vats. The vats were set up somewhere outdoors, usually at the edge of a vast lawn. Each vat contained lots of broken ice and, embedded in the ice, hundreds of tube-shaped terra-cotta containers filled with *kulfi*. Every now and then the *kulfi-wallah* would ease his arm into the vats and give its contents a knowing swish. *Kulfi* is not difficult to make at home as I have discovered in the years that I have been deprived of local *kulfi-wallahs*. All you need is an adequate freezer. (If you have an ice cream machine, you may use it for *kulfi*.) *Kulfi* is not made with cream but with reduced milk. It helps to have a very heavy pot with an even distribution of heat for boiling down the milk. A heavy, nonstick saucepan would also do.

Serves 6

2.25 liters (9 cups) milk
10 cardamom pods
6 tablespoons sugar
2 tablespoons chopped, blanched almonds
3 tablespoons chopped, unsalted pistachios

Bring the milk to a boil in a heavy pot. As soon as the milk begins to rise, turn the heat down, adjusting it to allow the milk to simmer vigorously without boiling over. Add the cardamom pods. The milk has to reduce to about a third of its original amount, that is, to about 750 ml (3 cups). Stir frequently as this happens. Whenever a film forms on top of the milk, just stir it in.

When the milk has reduced, remove the cardamom pods and discard them. Add the sugar and almonds. Stir and simmer gently for 2–3 minutes. Pour the reduced milk into a bowl and let it cool completely. Add half of the pistachios and stir them in. Cover the bowl with aluminum foil and put it in the freezer. (If you have an ice cream machine, you could empty the contents of the bowl into the machine and get it going.)

Put 6 small, individual cups, empty yogurt cartons, or a 900 ml (3$^2/_3$ cups) pudding bowl into the freezer.

Every 15 minutes or so, remove the ice cream bowl from the freezer and give the ice cream a good stir in order to break up the crystals. As the ice cream begins to freeze, it will become harder and harder to stir it. When it becomes almost impossible to stir, take the containers out of the freezer. Work quickly now. Divide the ice cream between the cups or empty it into the pudding bowl. Sprinkle the remaining pistachios over the top. Cover the cups or bowl with aluminum foil, crinkling the edges to seal them. Put into the freezer and let the ice cream harden.

carrot halva

Gajar ka halva

This is a lovely, fresh-tasting halva that makes the most of the natural sweetness of carrots.

Serves 4

6 medium carrots
750 ml (3 cups) milk
8 cardamom pods
5 tablespoons vegetable oil or *ghee* (page 28)
5 tablespoons granulated sugar
1–2 tablespoons golden raisins
1 tablespoon shelled, unsalted pistachios, lightly crushed
275 ml (1¹/₄ cups) heavy cream (optional)

Peel the carrots and grate them either by hand or in a food processor. Put the grated carrots, milk, and cardamom pods in a heavy-bottomed pot and bring to a boil. Turn heat to medium and cook, stirring now and then, until there is no liquid left. Adjust the heat, if you need to. This boiling down of the milk will take you at least 30 minutes or longer, depending upon the width of your pan.

Put the oil or *ghee* in a nonstick frying pan and set over medium-low heat. When hot, put in the carrot mixture. Stir and fry until the carrots no longer have a wet, milky look. They should turn a rich, reddish color. This can take 10–15 minutes.

Add the sugar, raisins, and pistachios. Stir and fry another 2 minutes.

This *halva* may be served warm or at room temperature.

Serve the cream on the side for those who want it.

creamy rice pudding

Phirni

As a child, there was nothing more comforting to me than to come home from school and find shallow terra-cotta bowls of this creamy dessert cooling in neat rows in the refrigerator, all lightly dusted with slivers of pistachios and almonds. Even though they were meant to be eaten at the end of the evening meal, my mother always filled extra individual bowls so that we could eat their contents as a quick snack.

Since the milk needs to be reduced somewhat, I like to use a wide pot – nonstick is ideal – which allows for quicker evaporation.

Serves 4–6

1 liter (4$^1/_2$ cups) rich milk

10 cardamom pods

3 tablespoons finely ground rice

6–7 tablespoons sugar

4 tablespoons slivered, blanched almonds

2 tablespoons finely slivered or finely chopped unsalted pistachios

Pour the milk into a wide, preferably nonstick, pot. Add the cardamom pods and bring to a boil without letting the milk spill over. Quickly turn heat to medium – the milk should simmer as vigorously as possible without boiling over – and cook, stirring now and then, for about 15–20 minutes or until the milk has reduced to 750 ml (3 cups).

Sprinkle the ground rice slowly into the pan, stirring as you go. Add the sugar as well. Cook, stirring now and then, for 7–8 minutes or until the pudding has thickened to a creamy consistency, turning the heat down a bit toward the end of this cooking time. Turn off the heat. Pick out and discard the cardamom pods.

Set a small, cast-iron frying pan over medium heat. When very hot, put in the almonds. Stir, shake or toss them until they are lightly roasted and turn golden. Set them aside.

Put the pistachios into the same hot frying pan and roast them even more briefly until they turn just a shade darker. Set aside.

When the pudding has cooled to lukewarm, stir the almonds into it. Ladle the pudding into 4–6 small ramekin dishes. Sprinkle the top with the pistachios and cover with plastic wrap. Refrigerate for 2–3 hours until cold and set.

mangoes

Good mangoes are among the best fruit on earth. They can be found in two basic forms, canned and fresh. The canned ones come sliced, or as a purée. I rarely serve the slices as I find their texture to be pathetically mushy but I do use the purée. I often chill it thoroughly, then swirl it into a bowl filled with double the amount of whipped cream and sprinkle some toasted almonds or pistachios over the top. It is a very simple dessert. Very refreshing too.

Fresh mangoes are another matter. If you ever see good ones (those with a strong mango aroma), such as the *alphonso* from the Bombay region, do buy them. Remember, though, that many grocers sell mangoes that are not fully ripe. Such mangoes may be ripened at home. Just wrap them individually in newspaper and then put them in a covered basket or cardboard box. Leave this container in a warm place (such as the kitchen) until the mangoes are ripe. A ripe mango should yield slightly when pressed. After the mangoes have ripened, they should be chilled, peeled, and sliced. Mangoes do have stones. So you have to slice around them. Do not throw the stones away before nibbling off all the flesh first!

spiced tea

Masala chai

This tea, flavored with cinnamon, cardamom, and cloves, may be served at teatime or at the end of a meal. I love it on cold, blustery days, with some Spicy Matchstick Potato Crisps (page 51) to nibble on the side.

Serves 2

600 ml (1¹/₂ cups) water

2.5 cm (1 inch) cinnamon stick

8 cardamom pods

8 cloves

175 ml (²/₃ cup) milk

6 teaspoons sugar, or to taste

3 teaspoons any unperfumed, loose black tea

Put the water in a saucepan. Add the cinnamon, cardamom pods, and cloves and bring to a boil. Cover, turn heat to low, and simmer for 10 minutes. Add the milk and sugar and bring to a simmer again. Throw in the tea leaves, cover the pan, and turn off the heat.

After 2 minutes, strain the tea into 2 cups and serve immediately.

index

Pages with illustrations are shown in *italics*.